THE AGILE START-UP

THE AGILE START-UP

QUICK AND DIRTY LESSONS EVERY ENTREPRENEUR SHOULD KNOW

JEFF SCHEINROCK
MATT RICHTER-SAND

WILEY

Cover Design: C. Wallace
Cover Image: Titamium © iStockphoto.com/ranplett
Cover Illustration: Łukasz Zaręba and Magdalena Busłowska

Published by John Wiley & Sons, Inc., Hoboken, New Jersey.
Published simultaneously in Canada.

Special thanks to the illustrators Łukasz Zaręba and Magdalena Busłowska.

Thanks to Craig Finster, Matthew Pierce, and Matt Levin for helping with illustration revisions.

For general information on our other products and services or for technical support, please contact our Customer Care Department within the United States at (800) 762-2974, outside the United States at (317) 572-3993 or fax (317) 572-4002.

Wiley publishes in a variety of print and electronic formats and by print-on-demand. Some material included with standard print versions of this book may not be included in e-books or in print-on-demand. If this book refers to media such as a CD or DVD that is not included in the version you purchased, you may download this material at http://booksupport.wiley.com. For more information about Wiley products, visit www.wiley.com.

Library of Congress Cataloging-in-Publication Data:

ISBN 978-1-118-54826-4 (Hardcover); ISBN 9781-1-11874448-2 (ebk);
ISBN 978-1-118-74472-7 (ebk)

Printed in the United States of America.

10 9 8 7 6 5 4 3 2 1

Contents

CHAPTER 2

MAKE IT FEASIBLE

CHAPTER 3

CUSTOMERS AND COMPETITION

CHAPTER 4

MAKING MONEY

CHAPTER 5

MARKETING

CHAPTER 6

TEAM

CHAPTER 9

BUILDING THE BUSINESS

CHAPTER 10

WHAT TO KNOW BEFORE YOU GO

Why You Should Read This Book

Despite the advantages today's entrepreneurs have, getting a company off the ground remains remarkably challenging. To be successful, you have to give it everything you've got—your heart and soul, your focus, and your life savings. Even then, the likelihood that you'll succeed is frighteningly low. But if you're one of the lucky few who manage to get your startup off the runway, building and running your own company will be one of your most rewarding and memorable experiences. Entrepreneurs live unique and fulfilling lives. In exchange for unreal and untold sacrifices, they get to live their passion every day and make a tangible difference in the world. If you are destined to become an entrepreneur, this book is for you. *The Agile Startup* will show you how to dodge painful, common, and *avoidable* mistakes and get your startup down the runway and in the air. Through the 170 startup strategies, you'll be exposed to the latest ideas, philosophies, frameworks, and best practices for entrepreneurship in today's fast-paced, hypercompetitive world.

The Agile Startup is not meant to be a comprehensive overview of how to start a business. Instead, it's filled with quick, actionable, timeless lessons from the trenches for soon-to-be founders or existing entrepreneurs. The lessons show you how to bob and weave with the market, get vital feedback, and build blockbuster products. The book will show you how bad assumptions kill companies, and why the most important thing you should do as an entrepreneur is to turn assumptions into facts as quickly as possible.

Most of the time-tested strategies have risen from the ashes of failed businesses, often the best (and hardest) way to learn. If heeded, they will increase your likelihood of success and reduce the time required to get off the ground. If ignored, you'll learn the hard way that history repeats itself. In the end, you'll have over 170 actionable strategies to help you navigate the startup minefield and start living your entrepreneurial dream.

The Agile Startup is for every kind of entrepreneur, from the aspiring entrepreneur just starting out, to the established early-stage CEO. You can read the book cover to cover, or focus on the strategies that apply directly to your current situation.

Want more? Get 33 bonus lessons not included in the print edition, along with other tools and resources from the authors, at www.agilestartup.com/bonus.

The hope is that *The Agile Startup* will be something you reference and learn from for many years to come. It was written to help you succeed on what will inevitably be one of the hardest and most rewarding journeys of your life.

Come join our community at www.agilestartup.com, and keep us updated on your journey!

The Entrepreneur's Life Cycle

From pre-idea to scale, there are six distinct stages that every
entrepreneur goes through. In an effort to maximize the value you
get from this book, we've stamped every lesson with one or more of the
six stages. Referencing the icons would be a good way to get through
the book quickly if you're strapped for time (like most entrepreneurs) and
want to focus on your current situation.

1. PRE-IDEA

In the *Pre-Idea* stage, you know that you want to start your own business
one day soon, but you aren't working on any specific ideas yet. This is an
exploratory stage, in which you scan broadly for opportunities. Your first
ah-ha! moment when an idea starts to take hold will graduate you to the
next stage.

2. IDEA(S)

Idea is the second stage of an entrepreneur's life cycle. You move past Pre-Idea when you start to dig into one or more ideas because you think they have potential. Rather than committing to any one idea at this stage, you're still very much in an exploratory mode and trying to ascertain the feasibility of an idea through interviews and conversations.

3. SOME WORK DONE

It is in the third stage, *Some Work Done*, that you transition from an exploratory mode into a deep dive of a single idea. It's in this stage that you begin to commit resources by building a prototype (or brochure) to test the idea and get meaningful feedback.

4. BUSINESS LAUNCHED

In the *Business Launched* stage, as you might have guessed, you launch your business! This is when your activities transition from feasibility to building. You're still learning along the way, of course, but your learning efforts are much more focused on business-building activities. This is where you put all of your weight behind the business, and sink all of your resources into it.

5. CUSTOMERS AND REVENUE

For most companies, there's a gap between officially launching the business and generating revenue. The *Customers and Revenue* stage represents the milestone of landing initial customers and revenue. This is a great step forward, but you're not out of the woods yet.

6. SCALE

The sixth and final stage is *Scale*. This is when you've finally found product–market fit, and you're having a hard time keeping up with customer orders. While this stage is no less frantic than the others, most of the venture has been de-risked. The final test is one of execution—can you scale the company quickly enough to ride the wave, or will it wash over you?

CHAPTER 1

Agile
Philosophy

From idea to sales, a startup's launch path is invariably convoluted and confusing. Regardless of industry or idea, successful entrepreneurs share a common philosophy that helps them navigate the tempestuous sea and build thriving businesses. The lessons in this chapter capture the philosophy of the Agile Entrepreneur and create a solid foundation to build upon. It will help you frame your thinking and maximize your discovery process.

There are two overriding themes that emerge in this chapter. First, the best entrepreneurs realize that they don't have all of the answers. They're able to walk the fine line between being focused yet agile, and visionary yet reactive. This crucial theme is carried throughout the book, especially in the next section on feasibility.

Second, founders understand that starting a company is not about dreaming, it's about doing. This is the biggest factor that differentiates the winners from the losers. Some people plan, others act. The best founders are quick to make decisions and then act immediately. They realize that few decisions are final, which means it's almost always better to act first and plan later.

As you read through this chapter, look for these themes and apply what you can to your startup immediately.

RULE #1

Rule #1 in entrepreneurship is *to have fun.* As Dale Carnegie said, "People rarely succeed unless they have fun in what they are doing." If you're having fun, it's immediately obvious to everyone around you. You spring out of bed in the morning instead of snoozing for an hour. You are constantly smiling, and grateful for even the smallest things. More importantly, having fun actually makes you a better entrepreneur. Enjoying the process makes it easier to commit wholeheartedly, and fully immerse yourself, both prerequisites to success. This will allow you to push through the hard days, fly past the boring days, and overcome the obstacles that every founder experiences. If you're not having fun, what's the point?

WHAT'S YOUR WHY?

Without a doubt, starting a company is one of the hardest things that you'll do in your life. In fact, most entrepreneurs looking back say that they wouldn't do it again if they knew how hard the road would be. Getting a company off the ground takes years of discipline, dedication, faith, and follow through. There will be months (or years) of total uncertainty, causing you to doubt that you can even pull it off. If you want to succeed, you have to keep moving the ball forward. All entrepreneurs encounter this backbreaking resistance to one degree or another, and most quit on the five-yard line. To make sure you see it through, **you better have one hell of a reason as to why you're starting this business,** and it needs to be more than just money. Perhaps you're trying to make the world a better place. Or maybe it's that the old way of doing things is too painful. Possibly you want to be in charge of your own destiny. Whatever your reason, you need to have an inspiring vision that will get you through the dark times and help you live by Rule #1.

What's your why?

YOU ARE WRONG

It's pretty much guaranteed that whatever solution you have in mind today, you are wrong and it will change. Only by going through a process of learning and discovery with potential customers, industry experts, suppliers, and partners will you arrive at the right solution. In battle, this is known as the fog of war. In business, it's the fog of startups. Just as no battle plan ever survives contact with the enemy, **no business plan ever survives contact with the customer.** The landscapes and minefields—in both—are constantly changing and evolving.

The process of cutting through the fog is called *customer development*, which helps you approach your market with an open mind. The key here is to be honest with yourself. It's all too easy to tell little white lies that allow you to ignore reality and stay in your comfort zone. What separates naïve dreamers from great entrepreneurs is an eagerness to grapple with reality and react accordingly. Of course, you have to start with what you believe to be the best solution, but your vision will undoubtedly change as you move forward—probably drastically.

When you admit that you won't get it right the first time, you immediately open yourself up to a process of learning and discovery. You seek input and feedback as you go through the customer development process. While the feedback won't always be what you want to hear, it is absolutely essential to finding product-market fit and building a thriving company.

HEAVEN . . . AND HELL

Building a successful business from scratch is nothing short of amazing. Think about everything that needs to happen to start a business in today's hypercompetitive world. Entrepreneurs have to do pretty much everything themselves—design logos, understand the law, find partners and employees, figure out the right product/service offering, analyze the market and competition, pray that there's actually a need, convince their families that the years of sacrifice will be worth it, cobble together a plan, find a location, assemble marketing materials, and on . . . and on . . . and on. It never ends. Founders take on unproven ideas that will require them to devote years of their lives, on the hope and prayer that there will be light at the end of the tunnel. But you never know what will happen, and over half of all new businesses fail within the first five years. **There's only one thing that you can be certain of—your startup journey will be full of incredible highs and devastating lows.** Land your first customer and life couldn't be better, or miss payroll and it couldn't be worse. All of this could happen in the same week. Being an entrepreneur is both heaven and hell. It's not for the faint of heart, but it's an amazing life if it's the life for you.

YOU GET ONLY 15,000 DAYS

Startups are riddled with momentous, dream-crushing risk. It's inescapable. It's the unfathomable risk that forces you to commit and put everything on the line when you start a business. Despite all of this, there's one risk that's in a league of its own—that you let the years of your life slip away and spend your time not doing what you love. Your working life is roughly 15,000 days long. The average entrepreneur is 37 years old, which means there are roughly 10,000 days of "work life" left. Most of your waking hours are spent not with your family, but at work. The hours you spend working are meaningful, yet most people slog away the best years of their lives at jobs that don't give them meaning. Entrepreneurs, on the other hand, defy convention and seize the day. They find something that inspires them and gives their lives meaning. While there's a minefield of risks and pitfalls in front of them, they never have to worry about the most important risk in life. Whether you're new to the startup game or a long-time veteran, congratulations for chasing your dreams and doing what you love.

THE ENTREPRENEURIAL METHOD

There's only one thing you can be certain of in a startup—nothing is certain. You don't know the right answer, and neither does anyone else. To be successful, **you must become a scientist and look at your startup as a science experiment.** The process of turning your uncertainties (assumptions) into certainties (facts) is remarkably similar to the scientific method. Startups are all about trial and error, and experimentation. Once your experiments are underway, stay open-minded, expect change, and react based on your findings.

There are five steps to the Entrepreneurial Method:

1. **Question**. Define the problem—what pain are you trying to solve?

2. **Observe**. Gather information and resources. Most of your time should be spent talking to industry veterans and potential customers.

3. **Hypothesize**. Make hypotheses about your assumptions on the problem, solution, market, channels, and everything in-between.

4. **Experiment**. Test your hypotheses to turn your assumptions into facts as quickly as possible.

5. **Analyze**. React to the outcomes of your experiments. If you got positive signals, keep moving forward. Test new assumptions or launch the company. If not, reconsider your assumption or abandon the project.

FOCUS ON PROBLEMS, NOT SOLUTIONS

At the most fundamental level, new products or services succeed because they solve problems in customers' minds. PCs helped eliminate tedious, time-consuming paperwork. Smartphones gave people an Internet connection anywhere in the world. Entrepreneurs are natural problem solvers—you started your company because you recognized a problem worth solving. You were fed up with the way things were done, and so you created a solution that would make peoples' lives easier. A common fatal startup pitfall to avoid is to focus exclusively on your proposed solution after launching. **You must maintain your focus on the problem, not your current solution, because your solution will undoubtedly change** in the coming months. As good as your idea may be, there are hundreds of reasons why it will change. You have to be adaptive, and the best way to do this is to focus on the problem rather than the solution. Write the problem down. Explore it with potential customers and partners. Resolve never to lose sight of the fact that you're focused on solving a problem, not forcing your solution on the market. By maintaining this focus, it will be only natural that you adapt and pivot toward the solution that has the best chance of being accepted by the market.

THREE REQUIREMENTS FOR SUCCESS

We always hear about the unequaled abilities of superstar entrepreneurs. Stories like these are juicy—the public and scoop-seeking reporters alike love them. This skewed media coverage makes it tempting to think some people succeed because they're blessed with special abilities. Talk to enough successful founders, however, and a different picture emerges. Their personalities are all over the map. Some are in-your-face outgoing, for example, and others are shy and reserved.

There are a handful of attributes that contribute to a founder's success, and they're what you would expect—vision, leadership, design skills, risk tolerance, and interpersonal skills, to name a few. While these traits may be necessary, they're not sufficient. At the end of the day, **getting a company off the ground comes down to three indispensable attributes: passion, sales, and follow-through.** If you're not passionate about your new venture, you won't be willing to walk through walls to make it work. Entrepreneurs are always selling—to prospective customers, partners, employees, suppliers, and investors. Finally, it's all about the execution and follow-through. It's about executing the plan and pushing through the boring, menial tasks to create something amazing. If you excel in these three areas, the rest will fall into line.

DREAMERS VERSUS DOERS

Too many would-be entrepreneurs are stuck in the land of fairy tales. Dreamers, blinded by the supposed genius of their ideas, fantasize about how marvelous life will be when they're running the show. As a result of misplaced motivation, they usually bounce from idea to idea, or focus on all the wrong things. They'll spend months writing a business plan (prematurely), perfecting website colors, printing fancy business cards, and so on. Of course you should dream, just make sure both feet are planted firmly on the ground. Dream where you'll be in a decade, and plan where you'll be next year. **Knowledge alone isn't power; it's potential power. Knowledge combined with action is power.** Take massive action in the direction of your dreams. Create a plan that outlines how to get from where you are now to where you ultimately want to be. Be honest with yourself, and determine as quickly as you can whether this is a viable business opportunity or a fantasy. If it turns out the idea won't work, *c'est la vie*. Get mad, get over it, and change your business model to make it work. If you're serious about building a business, be a doer, not a dreamer.

GET OUT OF THE BUILDING

Like all entrepreneurs, you think that you have all the answers. No, you *know* that you have the answers. You are wrong. What you have are assumptions, not answers. You have fiction, not fact. At the end of the day, feasibility is all about turning your assumptions into facts before you run out of cash. Only when you have the facts can you evaluate whether your business can actually make it. And, unbelievably, **there is only one way to convert fiction to fact in a startup—get out of the building and listen to customers.** You are on a search for facts, and learning should be your top priority. Unfortunately, you will never arrive at the truth by thinking harder. Google will never be able to give you what you're looking for. Staying inside the office and building more features will not sell more units. Through these customer conversations you'll get clues about the business, everything from right business model, to the customer pain points, to how and where to sell. But the only way to get this knowledge is to get out of the building and ask.

BUSINESS PLANS ARE WORTHLESS

Your business plan is worth less than the paper (or bytes) it's written on. Especially in the beginning, things are so fluid that it would be too time consuming to maintain any semblance of a professional, written plan. However, it's not about the plan; it's about the process of planning. By using a business plan as a framework to focus your efforts, you can collect answers to important questions that should help illuminate the path forward. As Dwight Eisenhower said, **"Plans are useless, but planning is indispensable."** You identify and plug the holes in your strategies and on your team, so don't think of your business plan as the final say on your business; think of it as a lighthouse, guiding your go-to-market strategy.

Using the business planning process in this way forces you to focus on the key issues, brings to light important dynamics, and helps uncover central questions that must be answered. Only after you have turned most of your key assumptions into facts, and your team rallies around a singular vision, does it make sense to spend time polishing your plan.

LET THEM STEAL IT

Some entrepreneurs refuse to share their ideas with others. A wide variety of excuses are offered to justify "stealth" mode, but the undertone is almost always that the entrepreneur was the first to think of the idea, and sharing it might jeopardize that advantage. There are so few genuinely new ideas that **you're more likely to get struck by lightning than you are to think of an original idea.** What's more, it's not about the idea; it's about the execution. To paraphrase Thomas Edison, startups are 1 percent inspiration, 99 percent perspiration. Think about how much time, effort, and energy you've put into your business so far. The person you're worried about would have to turn his or her life upside down to compete with you.

Being overprotective will prevent you from getting the crucial feedback you need to learn and evolve your thinking. Sharing and brainstorming with others is remarkably advantageous. Especially in the very early stages, almost every conversation will lead to epiphanies or new perspectives that drastically improve your chances for success. In other words, you immediately handicap yourself if you don't share your idea.

As an entrepreneur, your mission is to turn assumptions into facts as quickly as possible. This process begins with candid, open conversations about the customer pain and how you intend to solve it. Don't be shy— you have to get feedback to set yourself up for success.

EMBARRASS YOURSELF

If you're not embarrassed by the first prototype you put in front of a prospective customer, then you waited too long to launch. Your instinct will be to postpone your launch until your product is perfect. The problem with this approach is that you also delay vital customer feedback. By avoiding customers, you can easily waste months (or years) of effort building something that nobody wants. **The only way to figure out the needs of the market is to launch quickly and get in front of customers.** Get conversations started early and you'll be amazed at the epiphanies you'll have. It's not uncommon to discover that you missed necessary functionality, or that customers don't care about what you thought was indispensable. The sooner you know this, the less money you'll waste. The only way to learn is to ask, and the best way to ask is to put a prototype in front of an actual customer. If you're building software, make a prototype. Even if you mock it up with features that don't exist in the application, a prototype allows customers to see where you're going and give high-quality feedback. If you're starting a service-related business, create slick marketing materials and start pitching. However you do it, get in front of customers immediately. If you're not embarrassed, then you waited too long.

FAIL FAST—AND OFTEN

People learn best through trial and error, which is a nice way of saying that people learn through failure. Startups are no different. Let's say, for example, you assume that the only way to make your business feasible is to sell on a mass scale through distributors. Since this assumption underpins the feasibility of your business, you have to challenge this assumption. You throw together a prototype, and start calling on distributors. After meeting with five distributors, it's painfully obvious that there is no interest in your product. You can look at this as a massive failure. Or you can look at it as a learning experience. After all, you just figured out one way that it won't work, and picked up a ton of info from the interviews.

It sounds crazy, but to succeed you have to fail first—and often. As David Kelly, founder of IDEO, says, "Fail faster, succeed sooner." The chasm between reality and what you believe is often wide and deep. Only by trying something, failing, learning, and then trying again can you begin to piece together reality in the mind of the customer. Don't worry if you fall on your face . . . it's the best way to learn.

CONTAIN RISK AS EARLY AS POSSIBLE

Entrepreneurs are revered by the public and press as senseless risk takers. They're renegades who gamble everything on crazy ideas and irrational, futuristic visions. Yes, startups are soaked with risk. There are company-killing pitfalls and dangers everywhere, many of which you might not even know about. You could miscalculate consumer demand, miss the mark on your revenue model, ramp up your overhead too quickly, underestimate the time and cost of development, pick the wrong location . . . the list doesn't end.

But make no mistake—**great entrepreneurs contain risk, they don't seek it.** Great entrepreneurs reduce as much risk, as early as possible and constantly hedge against worst cases. A common way cutting-edge car companies de-risk their new products is through presales. Tesla presold $40 million worth of Model X's the day it was announced. How's that for containing risk?

Make it your mission to identify risk and attack it head on. Don't be afraid of risk; eliminate it methodically. Enumerate your assumptions in order of importance and knock them off, one at a time. The fewer assumptions you have to make going forward, the lower your risk. In the worst case, you identify a deal-killer and move on to the next idea, saving yourself months (or years) of struggle. In the best case, you greatly reduce the time it takes to build a thriving company.

FIRST, DECIDE WHAT NOT TO DO

Unfortunately, there are only 24 hours in a day. Even the best-funded startups are in a struggle against time. Despite working nonstop, deadlines will slip and opportunities will be missed. It's easy to get bogged down in day-to-day administrative tasks that don't really move your business forward. **Because there's so much to accomplish and so little time, you must execute on what matters most.** The best way to do this is to have a clear understanding of the core of your idea, which allows you to know what to do and, importantly, what *not* to do. You will be pulled in a dozen different directions as you get your company off the ground. It takes awareness and discipline to reject distractions that are opportunities in disguise, and stick to the plan. As tempting as it may be to split your focus, it's a recipe for mediocre execution and failure. One great way to initiate this process is to define what you are not. "I am not a consultant" . . . "We are not an incubator" . . . "We are not a manufacturer." Once you have a baseline of what you are not, it's easier to define what you are and use this as your North Star. First, decide what not to do.

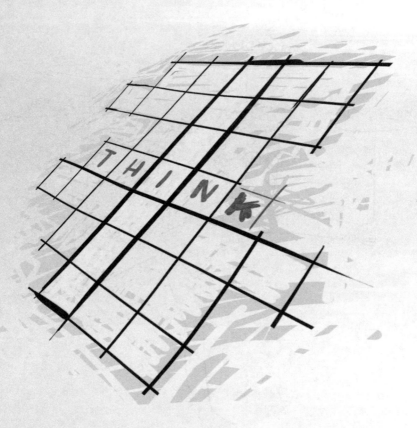

The Agile Startup

RULES? WHAT RULES?

The journey of a startup is daunting. Think about everything that you have to overcome, and you'll quickly see that the odds are stacked heavily against you. Every serial entrepreneur has a handful of gripping stories about impossible feats and lucky breaks. To overcome the odds and get your company off the ground, you'll have to tell a few white lies and bend the rules occasionally. Never break laws or put people in harm's way; but don't hesitate to be creative and push the boundaries. Bill Gates bluffed that he had written a game-changing piece of software, and tried to sell it to Altair. In actuality, not one line of code had yet been written when he pitched it. In fact, the first time he tested it was in front of the customer during the demo. This bluff launched Microsoft. Sometimes your only option is to ignore the rules and buck the system. For the entrepreneur, it's better to beg for forgiveness than ask for permission.

FOCUS—FOLLOW ONE COURSE UNTIL SUCCESSFUL

Being an entrepreneur is somewhat of a contradiction. You have to be able to scan for new opportunities, and focus completely on a limited number of projects at the same time. The temptation to change directions will inevitably rear its ugly head. It's hard to stick to your guns—people will question your vision, new ideas will come up, or a quick buck will be there for the taking. Of course, the temptation to change direction is usually the strongest when you're a few yards short of the goal.

Most entrepreneurs are genetically programmed to say yes to new opportunities. This isn't necessarily a bad thing. After all, it's your tendency to say yes that got you to where you are today. But it can also hold you back if you're not careful. **Every time you step off the path to your ultimate goal, you will have to retrace your steps to get back on track.**

The divide-and-conquer approach doesn't work with startups. Your resources are so limited that you have to focus everything you've got on your biggest opportunity. Follow one course until you're successful, and only then move on to the next project.

DON'T DRINK THE KOOL-AID

Many founders become so enamored with their businesses that they lose sight of the very customers they want to serve. They seem to forget that customers have the ultimate say whether the businesses lives or dies. Instead of confronting these unknowns head-on, they postpone or avoid the tough conversations. It's understandable—grappling with reality is scary, and means that you might have to admit that you're wrong.

Don't fall for your own sales pitch. You have to be honest with yourself—will people really pay for what you want to sell? Is the market big enough to make it a real business? Are you the person to pull it off? Ask the tough questions and don't take anything for granted. One of the best ways to do this is to list your key assumptions and share them with your advisors and partners. They will challenge you to ensure that you've covered all of the potential pitfalls.

Webvan burned through $1.2 *billion* before calling it quits. Don't be afraid to find business-killers, as it's better to find out early and adapt or move on than to waste your time and life savings on a pipe dream.

GET IN OVER YOUR HEAD

A big difference between large company managers and small business founders is the rate at which decisions must be made. As an entrepreneur, you have to make rapid-fire decisions constantly. You won't have all the information most of the time, either. It's easy to put off a decision to wait for more information, a mistake known as paralysis by analysis. To overcome this paralysis, realize that, especially with startups, decisions are temporary and nothing is set in stone. If you make a bad call, learn from your mistake, take a mulligan, and try again. Much worse is to avoid decisions and block your progress. **You're better off making a wrong decision now than not making any decision at all.** Make decisions quickly and react to what happens. Push forward constantly and challenge your team to make quick progress. If you're doing it right, you should feel slightly uncomfortable with your velocity. Anything less, and you're probably going too slow, and opportunities will pass you by. Get in over your head and see what happens.

THERE IS NO SILVER BULLET

There are no easy answers in the startup game. There's no immediate resolution or obvious solution. There's no single idea that, when it dawns on you, will guarantee your victory. Capitalism is so efficient that obvious opportunities are exploited immediately. **It will take years of blood, sweat, and tears to get your startup started. There's no way around this.** The only thing that's going to change the world is you. It's you getting the prototype ready at 4 A.M., four hours before a big demo. It's you schlepping it across town to meet with customers and get feedback on your latest release. It's you flying across the country to make that first big sale. It all comes down to you. But this is a good thing because all of the trials and tribulations you will go through are barriers to entry for prospective competitors. Starting businesses is a tough racket. It's about making your own luck by putting in the long hours and moving forward one step at a time. Don't look for a silver bullet because it doesn't exist.

IT AIN'T A PROBLEM 'TIL IT'S A PROBLEM

I t's easy to overthink and overanalyze issues with your startup when there are so many unknowns. Projecting into the future, your plan highlights key risks and potential downsides that you might encounter over the next few years. **Instead of worrying about things that might happen in the future, your overriding focus should be on taking the next step forward.** There's only one thing that you can plan on—nothing ever goes according to plan. The problems you worry about will rarely be the problems that you actually encounter. A common problem that web startups worry about, for example, is being able to scale to handle millions of users. Founders usually start worrying about this before they've landed their first user. As a result, the team spends weeks or months overbuilding to prepare for a flood of users. Only the flood never comes. Instead of being productive refining the app, learning from users, or addressing pressing issues, the team focused on solving a problem that wasn't yet a problem. When you start worrying about the future, realize that it ain't a problem 'til it's a problem.

LAUNCH TO LEARN

The foundation of *The Agile Startup* is that you don't have all of the answers; you have to get them from the market. You'll have hunches as to what the right answers are, but these are dangerous assumptions, not facts. You could be solving problems that no one cares about. **The best way to learn the truth and convert assumptions into facts is to launch your company.** Create a minimally viable product (MVP) that has the smallest feature set required to land your first customers. Your vision and early customer interviews will help you design the first version of the product. Then you can get an actual product in front of customers and react to their feedback.

Your intuition will tell you that everything needs to be perfect, so launching quickly will probably feel very wrong (at first). But your MVP is only the first release and not the ultimate vision. You will keep building, expanding, and developing your product. But now with customers in tow, you can be sure that you're solving real customer problems. Don't wait—the only way to learn is to launch.

RESOURCEFULNESS, NOT RESOURCES

Even the best-funded startups are resource-constrained. Entrepreneurs have to make every expenditure count. It's the nature of the game. Realizing this, the best founders don't fixate on their lack of resources; instead, they become masters of resourcefulness. Rather than worry about what you can't do, get creative and figure out a way to make things happen.

As frustrating as it may be, resourcefulness can work wonders for your startup. Being resource-constrained forces you to be more disciplined and build more intelligently. Some of the greatest public relations (PR) stunts ever devised resulted from a lack of resources. AirBnB made its first worldwide splash by renting the entire country of Liechtenstein for $70,000 a night.

One way that startups become resourceful is to partner with other organizations that already have what you need. To reach potential customers, for example, you can team up with an organization that already caters to your market. Hitch a ride with someone who's already done the heavy lifting for you.

Don't worry about your lack of resources. Instead, be creative and get resourceful.

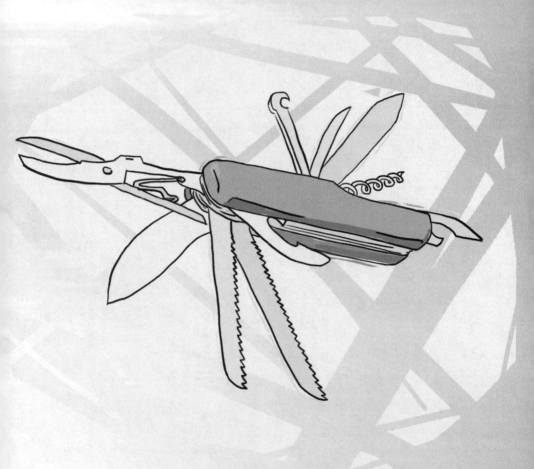

CHAPTER 2

Make It Feasible

A feasibility study is used to determine the viability of a new business venture. Commonly called a *business model* by entrepreneurs today, a feasibility study is simply a summary of the key components of a proposed venture. You will make literally hundreds of assumptions as you move through the six stages of entrepreneurship. These assumptions are directly linked to your risk of failure. The more assumptions you make, the higher your risk. As a result, your top priority has to be to turn your key assumptions into facts as quickly as possible. Without a doubt, this is the most important lesson in the book—to succeed, turn your key assumptions into facts as quickly as possible.

As you research the feasibility of your business with customers, investors, and partners, you'll find that many of your initial assumptions were wrong. This is to be expected—when you're innovating, you're venturing into the unknown, which forces you to make guesses about the future. The essence of entrepreneurship, therefore, is not nailing your business model at the outset. Rather, it's adapting to your emerging reality rapidly enough to survive. You have to be agile and make your business feasible. Every business has gone through these growing pains. Startups that can't adapt are quickly buried and left behind.

This chapter covers the most important feasibility strategies to help you learn, adapt, and make your business feasible.

ASSUMPTIONS

FACTS

The Agile Startup

IS IT FEASIBLE?

The point of a feasibility study is to determine whether you have a viable business. Whether a formal report or back-of-the-envelope estimate, feasibility is fundamental to analyzing new business opportunities. While there is no standard feasibility framework, there are two basic stages to any feasibility study.

The first stage is to put together a quick-and-dirty plan that outlines important feasibility factors such as the business model, price points, gross margins, distribution, competition, and so on. Realize that the plan doesn't have to be a written business plan . . . it doesn't even have to be written. The point here is to explore, at a high level, whether the business has any potential. The second stage is to enumerate and test all key assumptions. Since there's so little information at the beginning, you will be forced to make hundreds of assumptions. List these assumptions in order, with the most critical assumptions at the top. The main purpose of the second stage is to convert the make-or-break assumptions to facts. If you determine that the business is still feasible at the conclusion of this study, celebrate for a minute and then get back to work. If not, don't worry; most ideas won't pass the scrutiny of an objective feasibility study. At this point, you can **either adapt your idea based on the new information or think of another business and begin again.** Either way, get back to work.

ASS OUT OF U AND ME

Assumptions are elements of your proposed business that you believe to be true, but have not yet proven. As Oscar Wilde said, **"When you assume, you make an ass out of u and me."** In essence, assumptions are leaps of faith. They translate directly into risk, so the more assumptions you make, the riskier your startup. Examples include things like the number of visitors to your website that you expect will convert into paying users, a customer's average lifetime value, the length of the sales cycle, or even more "obvious" things like your price point. When you first start, you will make (literally) hundreds of assumptions. The point of a feasibility study is to convert enough assumptions into facts to demonstrate that you have a viable business opportunity. Your risk tolerance will determine how many assumptions are enough.

When exploring any new business opportunity, enumerate as many assumptions as you can think of. Put the list in order, from highest risk to lowest. Then, start converting the make-or-break assumptions into facts as quickly as possible.

There will be assumptions that you can't prove or disprove without launching, so learn as much as you can before launching. If you find that your assumptions are solid, keep moving forward. If not, don't ignore the warning signs. The next best thing to succeeding is failing fast, which allows you to conserve your time and capital for a business that will work.

THREE QUESTIONS YOU MUST ANSWER

As you study the feasibility of your new venture, it's easy to lose sight of the big picture. Fundamentally, starting and running a company is a straightforward proposition—you have to sell something to somebody. It's a common mistake to overthink every detail of your startup, but the truth is that you have to ask—and answer—only three questions:

1. **What are you going to sell?**
2. **To whom?**
3. **Why will they buy?**

Answer these three questions comprehensively and you'll understand what you need to know about your startup—details of the product or service, the size and characteristics of the market, your value proposition, how the competition stacks up, and so on. Ask these questions frequently to stay focused on what's important.

DOUBLE YOUR WORST CASE

Through the process of determining feasibility for your idea, you will explore and analyze every key aspect of the proposed business. Sometimes overoptimistic entrepreneurs include something intangible in their final analysis—a miracle. Common examples of miracle planning include things like going viral, astronomical conversion rates, unrealistic financial ratios, and inflated pricing.

Whatever your worst-case scenario is, double it. Count on the fact that your milestones will take twice as long to achieve and expenditures will cost twice as much as you anticipate. Once your business is operating, react immediately if things aren't playing out the way you expected. If, for example, you find that your customer conversions are 10 percent of what they should be, immediately revise your projections downward and reevaluate the business. **Accept the facts as they are, not as you want them to be.**

The viability of your business should be obvious, so plan extremely conservatively. Struggling to make the numbers work is a big red flag. Conversely, it's highly encouraging if the numbers still work after doubling your worst-case scenarios. Whatever you do, don't count on a miracle.

FIVE RISK FACTORS

Startup risks can be divided into five broad categories. The first risk is the *product risk*, which addresses uncertainties with the solution itself. Technology risk falls under this category. Product risk is high if you are trying to build a technology that doesn't yet exist. The second category is *market risk*. You hope that people will buy your solution, but how certain are you? Is this an established market that you are re-segmenting or is it an entirely new market? The third risk is *financing risk*. Undercapitalization is the number-one killer of startups. Do you have enough runway to get off the ground? Will you be able to raise adequate financing? Is it a capital-intensive business? The fourth risk is *competitive risk*. If you get traction, your competition will not idly stand by as you steal their market share. How will they react to your entry? The final risk is *execution risk*. Are you the team to actually pull this off? How much experience do you have in the industry, or with startups in general? Do you have a track record of success?

Rate each risk category on a scale from 1 to 10 (1 is no risk, 10 is monstrous risk). Once identified, take action to reduce that risk as quickly as possible. The name of the startup game is reducing your risk to increase your chances for success.

PRODUCT 1.0—A BROCHURE

Before you build a product, write a brochure. There are a bunch of benefits to getting early feedback with a brochure instead of a product. **Create a mock-up or spec sheet that takes one-thousandth the time and cost of building an actual product**, is quick to change, and results in feedback that's nearly as good. It doesn't have to be a brochure—anything tangible that potential customers can see or touch has the same effect. Mockups, wireframes, designs, and prototypes can all be used to get the point across in a realistic and convincing way.

The important thing is to be as visual as you can with potential customers. Giving them something to look at and play with makes it easier for the audience to "get it." Words get lost in the abyss. Images and prototypes are hard to misunderstand. Suddenly you're not talking about an abstract idea that your audience is likely to go along with (why wouldn't they?), you're pitching an actual product.

Being visual greatly helps you get an authentic reaction and objective feedback, so start with a brochure.

WHERE IS EVERYONE?

The Agile Startup

GOOD IDEAS, BAD BUSINESSES

Not all good ideas translate into good businesses. Many doomed entrepreneurs start their businesses on a whim—they see an opportunity for a one-off product that would make their lives better. Without carefully considering the business, they immediately set out to make the product, and try to build a business around it. There's more to building a thriving business than the idea alone. **Just because you can build something—or make a few sales—doesn't mean that it's a feasible business.** Think about everything that goes into creating a successful business—sales, distribution, marketing, product development, manufacturing, and much more. As important as the idea is, a myriad of those factors all contribute to a business's success. Before Groupon became Groupon, the website helped people mobilize and take action. Great idea, bad business.

Beyond the business dynamics, the idea itself can translate into a bad business. Most ideas aren't defensible. If you get any traction, you can expect a lot of competition, so if you can't fend off the competitors, then you'll have trouble becoming profitable.

When exploring your idea for a new venture, evaluate it as a holistic, defensible business opportunity, not just a great idea.

WRONG QUESTIONS
→ WRONG ANSWERS

To determine feasibility, you have to interview a lot of people. Interviewing, in fact, will take most of your time as you learn about how customers think and what they'd be willing to pay for. The questions you ask in these interviews will inform your entire strategy, making the ability to ask questions one of the most important skills of an early-stage entrepreneur.

The biggest mistake founders make when interviewing is that they ask leading questions, that is, questions that prompt your audience to respond in a certain way. When exploring revenue model, for example, a leading question might be, "Would you rather pay one time up front, or a monthly subscription?" The structure of this question forces the respondent to choose one or the other when it's possible that they wouldn't pay anything. Leading questions can constrain your interviewees and bias their responses.

Instead, ask open-ended, unbiased question like, "Is this something that you would pay for?" Try your best to ask open-ended, unbiased questions that result in actionable insights. **If you ask the wrong questions, you'll get the wrong answers.**

VITAMIN, PAINKILLER, OR CURE?

Always **think about your product or service in terms of the benefits it provides to its users.** Your solution is much more than the sum of its features. One way to evaluate your product is to consider how well it solves the pain for the customer. There are three categories that it can fall into—a vitamin, a painkiller, or a cure. Vitamins promise indirect, long-term benefits that address general health or minor problems. They are nice to have, but they won't wreck your day if you forget to take them. Painkillers are the next best solution, which are necessary short-term fixes to pressing issues. While more of a necessity than vitamins, they rarely solve the underlying issues. Finally, cures make the problems go away entirely. Customers' willingness to pay depends directly on their need for your product. They're often willing to pay significantly more for cures than vitamins. But cures are also harder to establish and defend.

If you expect to get significant traction, your solution should be a painkiller at least. Then, once established, be on the lookout for ways to better solve customers' problems to make your product that much more important.

CREATE MASSIVE VALUE

There's only one thing you need to know to build a successful company—you must create massive value for your customers. **Customers will trade their hard-earned cash for one thing only— value.** Therefore, you must have a deep understanding of what your customers need and how to help them get what they want. Formally known as the *value proposition*, there are three main components to value: the benefits gained from using your product, the target market, and the price relative to competitors or substitutes.

Realize that your value proposition is specific to each market segment. Your target market and follow-on markets likely have different value preferences, and you have to cater to each. The benefit that gets one customer to buy might create ambivalence in another.

Get to the bottom of all three aspects of your value proposition by asking a lot of questions and listening carefully. Vary your messaging and see what gets customers excited. Despite the formal definition, this isn't academic—what you understand to be your value proposition will become the foundation for sales and marketing efforts down the road. Nail all three and customers will beat a path to your door.

WHY WON'T IT WORK?

When exploring a new idea, you have to play devil's advocate constantly. It's too easy to fall in love with your concept and lose track of reality. A great way to challenge the business concept and question its feasibility is to ask, "Why won't this work?" As optimistic as you may be about your chances, **take an hour to brainstorm reasons that the business could fail.** Write everything down, and then separate this list of reasons into primary (key) risks and secondary risks. Once you have a polished list of key risks, take it to your advisors and industry experts to see if they agree with your assessment. At the very least, this will be a good opportunity to test how well you know the industry. The final list is a good gut check—do you feel comfortable with this level of risk? How do you plan to address the key risks? How much risk are you really taking on? A successful entrepreneur is not a risk seeker; she is a risk container. Is the risk contained enough to take the next step? If so, insert the risk list into your business plan, add to it when necessary, and always work to minimize your risk exposure.

SHOW ME THE MONEY

Talking someone out of their hard-earned money is a great way to determine the feasibility of an idea. In fact, selling is the best form of entrepreneurial market research. **What people say and what they actually do are often drastically different.** As an entrepreneur, you're the underdog, so it's natural for people to root for you. Asking for the sale instantly transforms the conversation from one of unwavering support to objective evaluation and feedback. No longer are you the heroic entrepreneur whom people want to succeed. Now you're another annoying salesperson. As a result, you're more likely to get honest feedback and objections, which will be invaluable to product development. If you can't get a purchase order, then you should try for a commitment in writing that your prospect will eventually pay for the product. It's not as good as revenue, but it's better than nothing.

The icing on the cake is that, by asking for the sale, you might actually land a few paying customers. The cash flow will be a big psychological boost. It's the best evidence you can have to prove to yourself, your family, and potential investors that this truly is a viable business.

DOES IT PENCIL?

The feasibility of a business is determined by its ability to make a profit. As obvious as that sounds, it's easy to overlook in the fever pitch of startup excitement. A quick and dirty way to figure out if an idea pencils financially is to **examine three figures: sales price, gross margin, and overhead.**

Gross margin is the sales price less cost of goods sold, or how much it cost you to make the sale. The overhead expense is the sum of monthly fixed costs incurred regardless of sales activity. For example, suppose you sell pocket protectors for $5 each, and that your cost for each is $0.50. Also suppose your monthly overhead—salaries, office space, utilities, and marketing—is $9,000 per month. Your gross margin is $5.00 minus $0.50, or $4.50 per sale. Dividing the monthly overhead by the gross margin gives you the volume required each month to break even. In our example, you would need to sell more than 2,000 pocket protectors each month to make a profit. Time for a quick sanity check—what's your plan to generate 2,000 sales each month? Is this realistic? Are you so sure that you're willing to bet your future on it?

PLAY DUMB

The importance of early interviews can't be overstated. Hidden in these conversations are the clues you need to piece together your startup puzzle. These clues will either confirm that you're on the right track, or save you years of unnecessary struggle.

It's important to know how to listen when investigating your idea. The point of interviewing prospective customers is not to impress people with your knowledge or sell them on your idea. Instead, **you need to get candid and honest feedback.** Entrepreneurs have a lot of trouble taking off their sales hat, which can result in useless, biased feedback. If you ask leading questions, you'll get loaded answers. Biasing your interviews is one of the easiest and most damaging mistakes you can make.

Turn off your charm and be as boring and dispassionate as possible. Act as if you couldn't care less. The less people think you care, the more likely you are to get honest feedback. You might even go so far as to say that you're doing some research for a friend. Play dumb and see what people say. Let them be the experts and encourage them to educate you. People will open up and be much more helpful.

TAKE A HAIRCUT

By now you know that you need to get your product launched as quickly as possible. It's easy to postpone the launch, and convince yourself that a polished product will generate more sales. But the more features you add, the longer it will take to launch, and the more time required to determine feasibility. Launching quickly will give you the feedback you need to iterate and improve on your initial idea, which will help you create something that people will actually pay for.

A haircut is a great way to boil down your product to only the most essential features. **List all of the features you believe are necessary to launch, and eliminate *at least half* of them.** Seriously. As impossible as this may sound, forcing yourself to eliminate features is the mentality you need to adopt to get to market quickly, win customers, drive revenue, and stay alive. Don't get bent out of shape—you're not killing the features forever. You're only putting them on the back burner until customers ask for them. Imagine all of the time you'll save, which can now be spent with customers, learning about the right direction to take the product.

IF YOU BUILD IT, WILL THEY COME?

A fundamental piece of any feasibility study is the *customer acquisition strategy*, or how you will land new customers. You should have a great answer to the question, "How are you going to get customers into your store or drive users to your website?" This is so important, in fact, that it routinely separates the winners from the losers. Often underestimated, many first-time entrepreneurs (consciously or not) adopt the *Field of Dreams* mantra, "If you build it, they will come." They won't. Even big companies like Disney make this mistake. They launched Go.com expecting the masses to come, but no one showed up. Just a few years after launch, Disney took a $790 million write-off and shut it down.

Today more than ever there is so much noise and demand for a customer's attention that it's next to impossible to stand apart from the crowd. **A solid customer acquisition strategy is one of the most important aspects of your go-to-market plan.** Once you have the broad strokes of a strategy in mind, challenge your most critical assumptions through quick, low-cost experiments that reveal actual conversion rates, customer interest, effective positioning, and competitive differentiation. Do what's necessary to get the data, but don't scale until you have a verified strategy to drive users and get customers. Having a compelling customer acquisition strategy will give you and your investors the confidence that when you build it, they actually will come.

BUYING CUSTOMERS

How hard is it to reach your target market? Do you have to search for customers or will they find you? The average dollar amount spent to land a new paying customer is called the customer acquisition cost (CAC). If you hire a salesperson who costs $1,600 each week and she lands four customers per week on average, your customer acquisition cost is $400. On the web, if you pay for Google Adwords at $2 a click and it takes 30 clicks to get a user to sign up, your cost is $60. Different market segments vary widely in how challenging they are for companies to reach. Some audiences are impossible to find, whereas others have obvious and cost-effective channels. **The harder it is to reach potential customers, the higher your acquisition costs will be.** As a startup with limited resources, you have to plan your initial targeting carefully because a high acquisition cost can quickly break the bank. Underestimating the CAC bankrupted eToys, a dot-com company valued, at one point, in excess of $4 billion. Try to estimate your CAC up front to see if it makes financial sense. If you find that the CAC is too high, experiment by either targeting different channels or different segments. The CAC is a vital startup metric for you to analyze and monitor continuously.

CLV >= 2 × CAC

Now that you know the acquisition cost of new customers you can compare that to the customer lifetime value (CLV). The CLV is the total amount of money that an average customer will pay you. For example, if you charge $30 per month for your service and the average customer is retained for 10 months, your CLV is $300. **If CAC > CLV, you won't be in business very long.** If CAC = CLV, then you won't make any money on these sales, and again, you won't be in business very long. This strategy might make sense in the short term to build a customer base, but it's not sustainable in the long run. The best situation, and a metric to work towards, is for the CLV to be at least double the CAC (CLV >= 2 × CAC). This cushion gives you the ammo you will need to expand your marketing efforts and sustainably build a solid customer base. Obviously, the more cushion the better. These metrics will be hard to know with any certainty before you launch, so make educated guesses and monitor your progress closely. The bottom line is that you don't have a feasible business if it's too expensive to reach your customer given your prices and margins.

CASH IS MORE IMPORTANT THAN YOUR MOTHER

Cash is king. The cash dynamics of your startup are often a make-or-break aspect of your feasibility study. There are two sides to cash, what you take in and what you pay out. The two should be evaluated independently. Since cash coming in is usually a distant dream at a company's founding, focus on the outflows. To illustrate the point, consider your sales cycle, or how long it takes to sell your product to potential customers. There are some businesses with months-long sales cycles. Imagine the cash implications of this long sales cycle—you have to cover the overhead for months while your team is burning cash, struggling to close sales. There are a bunch of similar cash-related activities that are easy to overlook but crucial to feasibility. **Poor cash management will bury your business.** Take each assumption in turn, consider the cash implications, and project out your cash requirements. How much cash do you burn before you get to breakeven? Adding up the monthly losses will tell you how much money you'll need to build the company.

THINK LIKE A VC

When exploring the feasibility of your business, pretend you are the investor. Actually, it's not that far from the truth—**you are about to invest years of your life, and most likely your life savings, into this high-risk venture.** You want to be sure this is the right opportunity. Among other things, an investor usually conducts at least a month of due diligence before making an investment decision. They will ask tough questions: Is the market large enough and growing? Why will customers buy? How big is this financial opportunity? Is this the right management team? How do they think about the product and industry? Ask these tough questions (and many more) of yourself. Does your idea withstand the scrutiny?

If you find this process difficult, find a savvy investor in your area and pitch him. In addition to great feedback, you'll be able take a step back and see how an investor would look at your business.

Like buying a house, starting a business is a very emotional process, and it's easy to lose sight of the fundamentals. Looking at your business like an investor will help you get into the proper mindset, so you can evaluate the opportunity dispassionately.

CHAPTER 3

Customers and Competition

I n this chapter, you will explore two important fundamental components of a winning business model—the market (customers) and industry (competition). Your startup must be different in a way that's important to your customers. Without meaningful differentiation, you're forced to compete on price, which puts your startup on death row.

Here, you'll learn how to use your competition to gain an advantage, how to break down a market, and why that's so important for customer acquisition.

Most importantly, this chapter gives you the opportunity to step away from your idea and take a broad look at your proposed battlefield. As Warren Buffett famously said, "When a management with a reputation for brilliance tackles a business with a reputation for bad economics, it is usually the reputation of the business that remains intact." No matter how good you are as an entrepreneur, it's hard to succeed if you pick a shrinking market or a cutthroat industry. Avoid the most common pitfalls and learn how to identify promising opportunities with the strategies presented here.

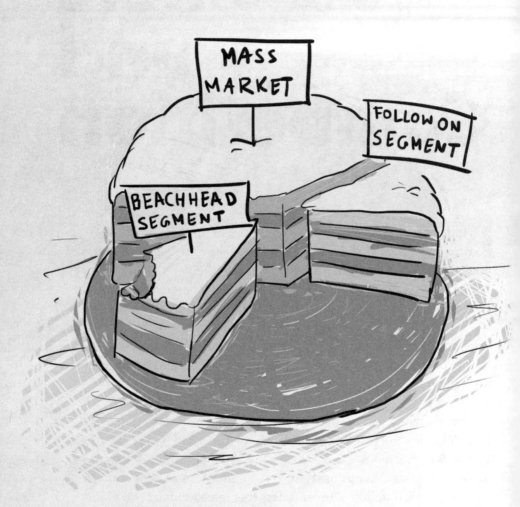

BREAK IT DOWN

When looking at the feasibility of a new idea, you have to break down the market. **Markets are usually sized in one of three ways: dollars, units, or customers.** Total available market (TAM) is a great starting point, which is the total size of a market opportunity—customers multiplied by average sales price. Other than knowing that you build a substantial company, TAM is pretty much useless. Much more useful are the serviceable available market (SAM) and serviceable obtainable market (SOM) metrics. SAM shows how much of the market your product has the potential to reach, and SOM is the percentage of the SAM that you will land as customers, factoring in the competition.

Once you have a holistic view of the market, segment it into groups of distinct customers. There are hundreds of ways to segment a market, making this much more of an art than a science. Hopefully, your product is different than the competition, so it will appeal more to certain segments of the market. Pick your target market based on which segment sees the most value in your offering. Breaking down your market will guide many essential business-building activities, so take your time and get it right.

RIDE THE WAVE

The typical startup story goes something like this: An aspiring entrepreneur grows tired of being inconvenienced in some way, so she creates her own solution. After proving her new solution works, she decides to make a business out of it. Usually, very little thought is given to the bigger picture or market trends. This is an opportunistic approach to startups. You can be successful doing this, of course, but there might be a better way. **Instead of diving right in with whatever opportunity slaps you in the face, try to predict the future.** What will the world be like over the next decade or two? Which industries will explode, and which will die? Read about current megatrends happening, and think about how you can ride one of those waves. As Wayne Gretzky put it, "You want to skate where the puck is going to be." By entering a large and growing market, you greatly improve your odds. This is why venture capitalists (VCs) insist on investing in large and growing markets. After all, a rising tide lifts all boats.

KNOW THY MARKET

There's a lot to be said for having industry experience on the founding team. Oftentimes, industries have quirks and ways of doing business that might not be immediately obvious to outsiders, but can make or break your business. For this reason, **unless you plan to disrupt an industry rather than compete in it, you need to have domain expertise on your team.** If your team doesn't have the right experience, get an advisor, partner, or employee to fill this hole. This will help in three key ways. First, an industry expert risking his reputation to join you will give you credibility. Second, the expert should have a solid network of industry contacts, which will help with everything from early feedback to strategic sales. Finally, and most importantly, this person will help you find the right product/market fit faster, which lowers your risk substantially. With a domain expert, when things go wrong, you'll be more likely to get to the root causes and understand why. While industry outsiders have unique perspectives, industry experience is a big plus.

WII.FM—YOUR FAVORITE RADIO STATION

WII.FM is everyone's favorite radio station—What's In It For Me? What you sell doesn't matter. Potential customers could care less about the features of your product or service. They only care about how it benefits their lives. Your product is a solution, designed to solve a problem in their lives. As such, when it comes to your market, **the main thing on your mind should be the benefits you give customers.** Are you entertaining them? Giving them bragging rights? Making them more productive? To understand benefits, you have to understand the pain that you reduce or eliminate.

Because benefits are so important, be sure to include both features and benefits when you do a competitive analysis. By including benefits, you'll get a much more insightful and actionable comparison. Obviously, different customer segments will have different priorities as to what benefits are most important to them, so a potential third dimension in your analysis would be the customer segment. From there, identify the segment that most values your differentiation—it often has the highest willingness to pay—and you've got your beachhead market.

TELL ME WHAT SUCKS

When first adopting a market-driven approach, it's tempting to think that prospective customers will be able to give you all the answers and tell you what they need. They're the ones with the pain, so they'll know the best way to solve it, right? Unfortunately, it's not quite that easy. Interviewing five prospective customers will probably result in 10+ completely different suggestions. If you blindly followed their suggestions, your product would end up confused and bloated. Of course, it's always helpful to understand a customer's pain and how she solves the problem currently. However, after this is understood, you should introduce your solution. Mock up your idea in the form of a minimally viable product (MVP) and put it in front of potential customers. In addition to getting general feedback, ask them what sucks. Ask them what they hate and will never use. This serves two purposes: (1) as long as you don't get defensive, this helps people give honest and unbiased feedback, which is crucial; and (2) it will give you the opportunity to cut the fat out of your MVP. Your mission is to get to market with the leanest possible product, knowing that you will iterate based on actual product usage. **Don't build more, build less and go as fast as possible.**

YOU CAN'T BOIL THE OCEAN

Once you're comfortable with the size of your market and the potential opportunity, it's time to **drill down and focus on one or two segments of the market with the highest potential.** Even if everyone under the sun is a potential customer, you have the resources to focus on only one or two core segments. You can't boil the ocean. If you want to build a social network of moms, for example, the best way to start is would be to target just one type of mom—like soccer moms—instead of all moms.

Your instinct will probably resist this—after all, aren't you limiting your chances for success? Don't think of it this way. People buy from companies they know and trust. Getting people to know and trust your company requires a lot of time, energy, and money. It's been estimated that it takes around $100 million to turn a product into a household brand name. Chances are you don't have this sitting in your bank account. However, while you can't reach all potential customers, you can reach a small segment of the market that sees the highest value in your product. You are basically doing the same thing big companies do, but on a much smaller scale. Plus, once you get traction and start generating revenue, you can always expand from there.

The Agile Startup

REFRAME THE COMPETITION

People are natural and creative problem solvers. If there are lingering problems of any importance, they'll usually find ways to reduce or eliminate them. The severity of the pain determines how far people will go to solve the problems. This is crucial to understand when considering your competition. You always have competition, whether they're direct competitors, who offer similar products, or indirect substitutes, that solve the same problems with different methods. Much more than your direct competition, the array of solutions in use defines your competitive set. The best way to arrive at a comprehensive list of competitors is to answer the question, **"What pain am I trying to solve, and how do people solve it today?"** This open-minded approach can lead to major breakthroughs. Southwest Airlines, for example, got its start by competing against cars, not other airlines. For the same price as a car trip, Southwest could get you to your destination in less than half the time. They reframed the competition. While airlines all compete for air travel, it's easy to forget that there are a bunch of ways to travel, including trains, rental cars, buses, and boats. How are your potential customers solving their problems today? That's your real set of competitors.

MAKE A COMPETITIVE MATRIX

When it comes to starting a new business, you can't overlook the competition. You have to know who you're competing against, and how you're going to beat them in at least one segment of the market. A common mistake is to underestimate the competition, particularly when it comes to new markets and innovative products. Naïve is the entrepreneur who denies having any competition. Whether direct competitors or indirect substitutes, you always have competition. And every competitor has features and offerings that appeal to different customer segments in different ways. The easiest way to visualize all this information is to create a competitive matrix that captures the companies/products along one axis and the features/benefits along the other. In the boxes of the table you use checkmarks or X marks to denote whether a competitor has a feature. If you want to add more detail, you can also write text in the box. The point of the matrix is to quickly **summarize who you're competing against, what features or benefits they offer, and your competitive advantage.** A matrix will help you highlight how your product is different and why it matters to the customer.

	MY DONUT	YOUR DONUT	THEIR DONUT
HOLE	✓	✗	✓
MARMALADE	✓	✓	✗
FROSTING	✗	✗	✓
CASTOR SUGAR	✓	✓	✗

DIFFERENTIATE OR DIE

A surefire way to fall on your face is to lack meaningful differentiation from the competition. **A startup that tries to win market share by copying an already established brand is dead on arrival.** If you're creating a new market, differentiation is already built in, but if you're competing in an existing market, then your product has to be unique in a very compelling way. Find a way to carve out a niche and appeal to the slice of the market that isn't satisfied with current offerings. Your differentiation will help spark distributor interest, get attention in the stores, give the press a reason to talk about you, and ultimately generate sales.

If you aren't different than the competition, the only way you can compete is on price. A startup competing on price is like a little leaguer going up to bat against Roger Clemens. Startups don't have the cash reserves or economies of scale to win that fight. And the only way to avoid competing on price is to create differences between you and your competitors that buyers actually care about. Differentiation is essential to premium pricing, so identify meaningful points of differentiation and make sure they're loud and clear.

COMPETITION IS A GOOD THING

When pitching their startups, first-time entrepreneurs often brag that they don't have competition. This boasting usually implies that they're onto a unique opportunity that's never been thought of before. News flash—there's no such thing as a new business idea. Capitalism is amazingly efficient at allocating resources and filling needs. If there is a latent need of a significant size, it has likely already been met. In other words, **if there really is no competition for your idea, then it's probably a bad idea.** Competition is a good thing. Not only does it establish that there is a market, but you can learn valuable lessons from your competitors. In fact, if you take a look around, most industry captains were not first to market. Instead, they were fast followers that used the lessons learned by first movers to catapult their own success. Granted, while incredibly rare, it is possible that you actually don't have any direct or indirect competitors. If this is the case, you better have a bulletproof story as to why you believe this market exists and how you're going to create it.

The Agile Startup

FOLLOW THE LEADER

When first starting out, you have to de-risk your startup by eliminating as many unknowns as early as you can. The way the industry works is one of the key unknowns to focus on, as there are often unspoken rules or norms that will heavily influence your strategy. Being aware of these nuances will improve your chances for success and help to minimize course corrections. For example, let's suppose that you have a new technology that you want to license to industry manufacturers. You then spend six months building the business around a licensing strategy, only to find out that the manufacturers have never licensed a technology before and won't work with you. Oops. Or, suppose you notice that a lot of restaurants don't accept credit cards. You set out to create a robust credit card payment system, only to find out that they like being cash only because of the tax benefits.

Industry details fundamentally impact your venture, so **learn as much as you can about how your industry works before you launch.** Talk to suppliers, distributors, industry veterans, competitors, and anyone else in the industry. There are times when innovation is good and times when you should follow the leader.

FAST FOLLOWERS FINISH FIRST

Entrepreneurs always want to be first to market. There's a sense of security about being first and not having any competitors to worry about. First-time founders often brag about the lack of competition to potential investors, and try to demonstrate that they will dominate the market by virtue of being first. Unfortunately, the idea that you gain an advantage by being first in a market is wildly misleading. **The companies that eventually dominate new industries are almost never first movers; they're the fast followers.** Think for a moment of as many Fortune 500 companies as you can. How many of them were veritable pioneers of the industry and how many were fast followers? Google, Microsoft, Apple, GM, eBay, and Walmart—all fast followers. Fast followers are companies that are not the first to market but close on the heels of the first movers. It's like NASCAR—the race usually comes down to the last few seconds, when the drafting car uses the car in the lead to build momentum and win the race. Isaac Newton said, "If I have seen further than others, it is by standing on the shoulders of giants." Think of your competitors' strategies as free advice, and stand on their shoulders.

So don't worry if you are not first to market. Use your delay as an advantage to learn everything you can about the marketplace dynamics, and then out-execute them.

THEIRS

YOURS

The Agile Startup

10× BETTER

When entering an established market, you have to worry about switching costs, or the costs required for a customer to switch from a competing product to yours. These costs vary based on the nature of the switch, whether they're intangible (brand to generic) or tangible (cash spent to switch database vendors). When starting out, think about the switching costs you will ask customers to make, and why it makes sense for them to buy your solution despite the extra expense. Some companies go so far as to pay the switching costs to get customers to change.

When thinking about switching costs, one rule of thumb is that your value proposition needs to be at least ten times better than the competition. For example, if you introduce a new email program with better spam technologies, it needs to be 10× better at blocking spam. If you want to start a consulting business, you've got to be 10× stronger in your area of expertise.

Ten times better can be hard to quantify, so just make sure that your offering needs to be significantly better. If it's marginally better, people won't switch. Regardless of the product or service, don't rest until your value proposition dwarfs your competition.

YOU NEED A MOAT

A moat is a deep, broad ditch that surrounds a castle and provides it with a preliminary line of defense. In their heyday, moats rendered the enemies' most effective weapons useless. **You need a moat. In other words, you need a sustainable competitive advantage.** It's possible to start a business without a moat, of course, but it makes your life a lot harder. The problem is that as soon as you're successful, you can expect company. Remember the hundreds of Groupon copycats? With a moat, you can seize the advantage by keeping enemies away and customers protected.

How do you create a moat? There are many forms of barriers to entry, including intellectual property (patents), know-how (trade secrets), speed of execution, brand awareness, cost advantages, government protection, and distribution rights. The most commonly employed technique is patent protection. With the right patent protection, the smallest company can hold Google or Microsoft at bay. If you don't have much of a moat right now, brainstorm ways to create one and work it into your plan. Down the road, you'll be glad you did.

ZERO DEGREES OF SEPARATION

It shouldn't be a special occasion for you to talk to your customers. They are your lifeblood, so get close to them and understand what's happening on the front lines of your business. Making a habit of talking to customers provides unequaled and necessary feedback. You'll follow trends in your industry, understand your customers' problems intimately, and be able to identify your weaknesses early. Blockbuster is one of the best examples of what happens when you bury your head in the sand and ignore customers. It took the competitors nearly a decade to erode Blockbuster's market share, so there was plenty of time to react. Yet the executive team didn't take the competitive threats seriously. Had management listened to customers, it's highly unlikely they would have missed the transition to the Internet and streaming.

You must always improve your offering to stay competitive. Customer appetite shifts like the wind. By keeping zero degrees of separation with customers, you'll be able to predict changes in demand and get ahead of the curve.

An average customer interview takes less than 10 minutes, so set aside some time every week to meet with customers. One meeting a week is often enough. Alternate between current and past customers to gain a solid understanding of why people prefer you or your competition.

CHAPTER 4

Making Money

You go into business to make money. It's as simple as that. It doesn't matter if you are opening a sandwich shop or starting the next Google; you can't stay in business long if you don't make money. Heck, even nonprofit organizations need money to survive.

This chapter deals with all aspects of making money, from the best ways to finance your business to building a financial model. You'll learn important strategies on how to stretch your bank account, why the first dollar you earn is the hardest, and the best way to forecast your revenue in the years to come. You might prefer to drag your nails on a chalkboard than think about this stuff, but you can't be a well-rounded entrepreneur if you don't understand what drives your bottom line.

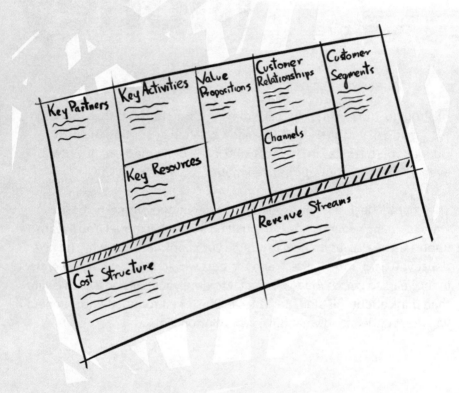

WHAT'S YOUR BUSINESS MODEL?

It's easy to get confused with academic definitions of *business model*, so let's put it in the simplest of terms—**a business model is how your business makes a *profit*.** Note that's profit, not simply revenue. If you want to focus on revenue only, that's what's known as a *revenue model*. This difference is important because there are many considerations that you should take into account other than revenue. You have to factor in the cost of creating the sale. Did you have to buy the inventory before you could sell it? Did you have to pay a big commission to a salesperson? You also have to factor in your overhead expenses. Do you need an expensive storefront, or can you get by with a website and home office? The questions that have to do with the financial dynamics of your business combine to create your business model, and indicate how lucrative your venture can be. There are a few useful tools you can use to help you through the process, such as the Business Model Canvas or the Lean Canvas. All aspects of your business have financial implications, so make sure you've got all the bases covered.

THE BEST SOURCE OF CAPITAL

Too many entrepreneurs are obsessed with investors. These kinds of founders are easy to spot—when you ask them how their businesses are going, a normal response would be something like, "Great, we just raised another round of financing!" Unless you're in the fundraising business, raising capital is not a business milestone. You're in business to make money, not raise capital. Fundraising is a full-time job and significant distraction when you're trying to build a business. Of course, there are times when your business will need a significant capital infusion. But by the time you're ready for this, investors will be chasing after you, not the other way around.

Instead of worrying about investors, **focus on profitable growth as the primary way to fund your company.** There are a lot of ways to do this. Instead of spending the next two years building a cutting-edge platform, what can you build in the next month or two that solves the same problem and starts generating revenue for you immediately? Is it possible to consult for the same customers now and start building strong relationships, so they'll support your first product? Profit is the best source of capital, so focus on making money.

HOW DO YOU MAKE MONEY?

Not to be confused with a business model, **your revenue model is how your company makes money.** There are dozens of potential revenue models, including subscriptions, product sales, data sales, lead generation, advertising, licensing, freemium, and fee for service.

Google's primary revenue model is selling advertising on its search pages. Walmart's revenue model is product sales. But dig a little deeper you'll quickly realize that Google and Walmart make money a lot of different ways, not just through advertising and product sales. A hybrid revenue model is often in order. But don't get distracted early on—focus on your core (the tree trunk) initially, and slowly branch out from there.

So what revenue models should you start with? Unless your differentiator is the way you charge customers, follow the leader and mimic the industry leaders. It's probably too risky to try to change the traditional business model *while* introducing a new product to the market.

Clearly understanding how your business makes money is crucial. Don't fall into the temptation of glossing over this. You're much more likely to stay alive and fight the good fight if you have a revenue model from the beginning.

GROSS PROFIT MARGINS

One of the most important financial metrics you need to understand is your gross profit. **The *gross profit* is the difference between the revenue and the cost of making a product or providing a service.** For example, if you sell a widget for $10 that costs you $4 to manufacture, your gross profit on each unit is $6. Gross profit is more commonly expressed as a percentage of revenue, which is called gross margin. In this case, the gross margin on your widget is 60 percent ($6 gross profit/$10 revenue). There are two ways to improve your gross margin: increase unit revenue or decrease cost.

It almost never makes sense for a startup to compete on price with low-margin products. Your competition can tap into its war chests to outspend you. Instead, look for a differentiated product that will allow you to charge a premium, resulting in high gross margins.

Gross margins are crucial for startups because higher gross profit creates a financial cushion, which pays your overhead, gives you freedom to experiment, buys you more time, and increases your margin for error. For a startup, gross profit equals survival.

PREFER VARIABLE TO FIXED

There are two kinds of costs—variable and fixed. Variable costs are those that increase or decrease along with a specific activity. Fixed costs, on the other hand, are those that are incurred on a routine basis, regardless of business activity. For example, consider salaried employees versus commissioned salespeople. An employee on salary will be paid every month regardless of the performance of the business. This person's salary is a fixed cost. Conversely, a salesperson paid 100 percent commission is a variable cost because he or she gets paid only when a sale is made.

Startups should always prefer variable costs to fixed costs. Hire independent sales reps instead of salaried employees. Work with a contract manufacturer instead of building your own manufacturing plant. Outsource billing, sales reports, and inventory to an accountant instead of bringing on a salaried CFO. Hire a PR firm based on performance, not retainer.

If you run out of money, you're dead in the water. **The fastest way to run out of money is to take on too many fixed costs.** So develop a strong preference for variable costs when building your company. The main secret of survival is to keep your overhead as low as possible, for as long as possible.

GO BOOTSTRAP YOURSELF

You *bootstrap* your business when you start and grow it without outside capital. The vast majority of companies started in the United States are bootstrapped. Why bootstrap? Most new companies can't generate the returns to get investors excited. Furthermore, many entrepreneurs avoid bringing on investors until absolutely necessary. While an injection of capital can be a godsend, investors can distract you from building your business. Fundraising is a full-time job, and managing existing investors can be a headache. **The day you take an investment is the day you commit to selling your business.** By bootstrapping, especially early on, you stay in the driver's seat. You can't always bootstrap at the outset, of course, but it's worth the extra effort.

Bootstrap-friendly businesses are those that can get to revenue quickly. You have to get rid of distractions that don't get you to revenue while bootstrapping. Revenue will keep you alive and able to grow.

If you plan to bootstrap, make sure you know how much money it's going to cost to get to profitability. The last thing you can afford is to run out of money.

The Agile Startup

THE FIRST RULE TO MAKING MONEY

Here's an obvious truth: You can't make money until you have something to sell. If you have a website that's half-built, or a product still under development, there's no way to generate revenue. **Each day you spend in product development is another day that you're not selling anything, which is one day closer to going out of business.** This is why the minimum viable product (MVP) is so powerful—build only what you need to get out of the building and start engaging with customers. Make your offering "good enough," and then start selling it. The longer you delay, the longer it will take to start making money, and the harder it will be for your business to survive.

New entrepreneurs frequently overlook the fact that if you want to make money, you have to have something to sell. Releasing your baby into the wild is never an easy thing to do. You've probably made significant sacrifices to get to this point, and the potential rejection looming around the corner is scary. But that's also why you're going to succeed—you're willing to put yourself out there and make it happen.

THE FIRST DOLLAR IS THE HARDEST

When it comes to personal wealth, people always say that "the first million is the hardest." With startups, the first dollar is the hardest. There are so many things that can go wrong. Making your first sale—no matter how small—is a significant achievement.

Earning your first dollar helps in a variety of ways—it gives you feedback from the market, the cash flow extends your runway, and it shows you who will buy and why. This is all valuable, but the psychological boost is probably the best part of your first dollar. Getting your first customer can take months—or years—in product development. The buildup to launch is always a trying time, riddled with uncertainty and doubt. Getting to that first sale gives you the confidence you need to keep going.

The vast majority of founders say that they wish they got to market sooner. Do everything you can to quicken your pace to market and get that first sale under your belt. After all, that first dollar is always the hardest.

BOTTOMS UP!

A key component of any business feasibility analysis is the financial projections. These projections will reveal the financial feasibility, scale, and investment required to get your business going. A common mistake is to create these projections from the top-down, rather than the bottom-up. A flawed approach, top-down projections are made when the entrepreneur takes a percentage of the whole market without justification. For instance, a top-down revenue projection might say that by capturing 2 percent of a billion dollar market, the company's revenue will be $20 million per year. This is the wrong way to go about it. Instead of guessing a percentage based on the total market size, build your case from the ground up. With a bottom-up approach, each sale must be justified and tied to a business activity. You can tie sales to traffic to your site, a sales team, joint ventures, or advertising costs. To project the revenue of a sales team, for example, calculate how many calls a salesperson can make in a day, the percentage of those calls that result in sales, and the resulting number of sales made in a month. Multiply this total by the number of salespeople and you have successfully completed a bottom-up sales projection.

Whenever you're projecting into the future, build your case from the bottom-up and you'll have a solid and realistic foundation to stand on.

BUILD A (BAD) FINANCIAL MODEL

Yes, your financial projections will be wrong. But that doesn't get you off the hook. **A financial model is valuable due not to its accuracy, but because building one forces you to think through every nook and cranny of your business.** All of your assumptions will be quantified in your model, helping you determine whether your business, as you currently envision it, has potential or not. Often, businesses that make sense in the abstract are unrealistic when modeled out. Plus, now that you have a financial model, you can use it to manage your business. You can update your assumptions as you collect more data, and get instant feedback on how these changes affect your bottom line.

Because your model is so important, it would be a mistake to use a template. You need to go through the process of building it yourself. You need to know what's going on under the hood, so you can explain how it works, and fix it if something breaks.

A financial model that incorporates all of your assumptions will help you take a holistic view of your business's dynamics. The financials are where the rubber meets the road in business. So go ahead and build a bad financial model. It's not the inaccurate projections that count; the important thing is the process.

HOW MUCH RUNWAY?

One financial number that you should always have in the back of your mind is how much runway you have left. **At your current cash burn rate, how many months can you survive before you run out of money?** Shoot for 18 to 24 months of runway at all times so you can focus on your business without worrying too much about money.

Calculate the runway left by dividing the money in the bank by your loss at the end of the money. For instance, suppose you are losing $10,000 per month, and you have $100,000 left in the bank. You have 10 months of runway left ($100,000/$10,000 per month = 10 months).

There are three things you can do to lengthen your runway: generate more revenue, lower your expenses, or raise more capital. If you increase your revenue and lower your costs, resulting in a $2,500 loss per month, then you've just increased your runway to 40 months ($100,000/$2,500 = 40 months).

Undercapitalization is the number one reason small businesses fail, so make sure that you always have enough runway to get your startup's wheels off the ground.

KNOW YOUR DO-OR-DIE NUMBERS

Every business has its make or break financial assumptions. **Also known as key performance indicators (KPIs), these do-or-die figures are the drivers of your business.** A web company's KPIs might include the conversion rate (number of visitors who convert into customers) and average time spent on the site. A restaurant business might focus on the time it takes to turn a table, or the average ticket size. As your company grows, your financial drivers will determine your success. Neglecting them will result in lost potential, or worse.

Drivers vary by industry. If you're not sure what your KPIs are, start by looking at industry reports. Read the 10-Ks of public companies in your industry and pay attention to what its managers focus on. Another great way to determine which indicators will most impact your business is with your financial model. Analyze the sensitivity of your inputs by testing each at different levels. The inputs that drastically affect your revenue or profit are likely your KPIs. Once you figure out you KPIs, make sure you know your numbers cold.

CHAPTER 5

Marketing

At the most fundamental level, marketing is the process of creating and keeping customers. Peter Drucker said, "Marketing is the distinguishing, unique function of the business." Marketing also happens to be one of the hardest things to get right in business, making it a common startup killer. Think about the thousands of amazing products and companies that didn't survive because they couldn't figure out how to get customers.

Your product can have winning differentiators, but so can your marketing strategy. Undoubtedly, marketing should be as important to your startup as product development. It's where the rubber meets the road. This chapter will show you quick and effective marketing strategies designed specifically for cash-strapped startups. Learn how to position your company and write copy that sells, and why creating two versions of the same product can be a winning strategy.

LUCK IS NOT A PLAN

At the most fundamental level, marketing is the process of converting unaware people into paying customers. Of all your activities, landing new customers is the heart and soul of your operation. Simply put, without customers you don't have a business. Since they're so important, your marketing assumptions should be the first that you de-risk. It will be tempting to set them aside as you build the business, but that's a mistake. You can't start a business without also knowing how you will land new customers.

There are several customer acquisition factors that could drastically affect your go-to-market strategy. You might discover that an assumed sales channel has specific requirements that will impact product development. Or perhaps you'll find that the cost of reaching your target market is astronomical. The earlier you explore these make-or-break assumptions, the more options you have and the better your chances for success. **Saying you're going to worry about customer acquisition later, that they'll come if you build it, is akin to saying that your plan is to get lucky.** While you do need luck on your side, don't make it the backbone of your plan.

WHAT'S YOUR POSITIONING?

Positioning is the process of creating a unique perception of your products, in the mind of the customer, as compared to your competition. **A positioning statement is the best way to succinctly capture the customer perception you're trying to create.** It conveys the core target of the product, and how you want customers to view your brand. A positioning statement is not a tagline or slogan, which is crafted to generate sales. Rather, a tagline or slogan is derived from the positioning statement. Use one of the following formats to write your positioning statement:

V1: <Product/Service/Company/Person> is the one <your category> that provides <your target customer> with <your key benefit> because <reason to believe you can deliver the benefit>.

V2: For <your target> who wants / needs <reason to buy your product/ service>, the <your product or service> is a <category> that provides <your key benefit>. Unlike <your main competitor>, the <your product/ service> is <your key differentiator>.

Once written, present your statement to prospective customers and industry veterans. Does your positioning create a unique perception? Are you sufficiently different from the competition, in an impactful and meaningful way? It will probably take a few revisions to nail it.

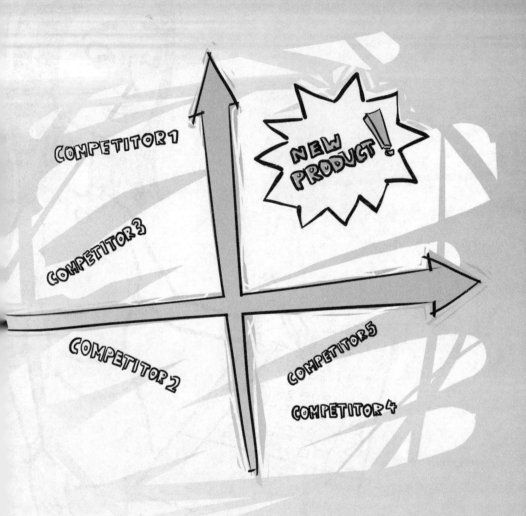

HOLD THE PRESSES

O ne common startup marketing trap is the lure of the press. A feature in the *New York Times* or an appearance on *Oprah* is considered the holy grail of publicity. But there are a few things you should know about publicity before you run out to hire a public relations (PR) firm.

You don't have any control over the messaging, and you're stuck with the perception created by significant media coverage. Because of this, it makes sense to make sure that you've got the product and experience nailed before starting a major press push. Getting press too early will greatly reduce your ability to change and adapt.

The return on investment of PR campaigns is highly uncertain. Most good PR firms charge between $5,000 and $10,000 per month. Six months with a PR firm can be an investment of as much as $60,000. That's a lot of money considering you don't have any guarantees. Will people actually buy your product or sign up for your service because you were quoted in the *New York Times*?

For most startups, this uncertainty makes early PR more of a lottery than a sound business strategy. Don't go to the press until you're ready.

OLD MEETS NEW

There are two kinds of markets—old and new. The computer industry is a mature and established market, whereas cloud computing is nascent and emerging. Your offering will either blaze a new path into the wilderness, or it will go to war with industry incumbents. Although the difference between the two might not appear important at first blush, it calls for fundamentally different marketing approaches. If you're venturing into the unknown, education will be your top marketing priority. You have to teach prospects how your product will make their lives better. Think about social networks in the early days—most people just didn't get it. Conversely, if you want to compete in an already established category, it's crucial that you differentiate your offering in a way that speaks to an underserved segment.

From a startup perspective, the most important thing to realize is how expensive both can be. Educating customers takes time and it's easy to burn through a marketing budget and come out on the other side empty-handed. Similarly, overcoming brand loyalty and stickiness in an existing market can be frustratingly difficult. **Know what kind of market you're entering, and don't underestimate how expensive it will be to convert customers.**

SELL WANTS, BUT DELIVER NEEDS

Consumers buy on emotion. Women buy beauty products to look like the models in advertisements. Men buy fast, expensive sports cars because of how they think they'll look driving them. While people buy on emotion, they also justify with reason. Purchases are usually rationalized after buying decisions have already been made. **To sell successfully, you need to understand your customer's mindset—both emotional and rational.** First, ask what their emotional triggers are. What gets them motivated, and what scares them? Then think about how your product delivers long-term value.

Marketing that leads with emotion and justifies with reason drives sales. Emotions can be tricky because they are short-lived, so make sure that you deliver real value. The way to do this is to sell them what they want, and deliver what they need. If you're marketing a fitness program, sell six-pack abs or a sexy beach body. These emotionally charged ads will get people to buy. But then deliver a comprehensive fitness program that delivers immediate value. Eventually customers will get a six-pack, but in the meantime they're happy with the value of the program. Sell wants, but deliver needs.

HOW CAN I HELP YOU?

We all like talking about ourselves, and why not? But when you or your ads are selling to a customer, the focus needs to be on them, not you. Companies focus mistakenly on the features of their products, instead of the benefits gained from using them. The problem is that prospects don't buy features or products, they buy benefits and solutions. Every product has to solve a problem.

Take all of your features and translate them into benefits for the customer. Then start your sales presentation by asking, "How can I help you?" **Make the discussion about their problems and desires, not about you.**

Focus on benefits, not features. If you're selling information technology (IT) consulting services, don't pitch a prospect about system integration, new applications, or your experience. Instead, talk about the money they'll save, and how much more productive they'll become. If you're placing an ad for a new scooter, don't brag about the engine size, the brake system, or the trunk. Instead, show how your scooter can save gas money, make them safer than other motorcycles, and make their commutes more convenient.

The Agile Startup

TURN $1 INTO $2+

Advertising is an investment. **As a startup with limited resources, you need to get a quick return on your advertising investment.** That is, you better get customers from your advertising spend, or you'll run your company into the ground before you can say the letters "I-P-O." You don't have the resources to waste money on advertising that isn't working.

While it isn't always black and white, an easy metric to help you determine whether your advertising is working is whether you are able to turn $1 into $2. Does every $1 you spend come back to the company as $2 in sales? If not, move on to the next advertising channel and keep experimenting. Repetition is the key, of course, so don't bail immediately if you don't see results. However, you should be able to ascertain relatively quickly whether a channel is working. If not, don't linger for too long. There are hundreds of ways to reach customers these days, so try another channel.

Also, don't settle for turning $1 into $1. As tempting as *any* revenue may be, $1 isn't enough to build your business. You need profitable revenue to fuel growth.

DO IT TWICE

The market has the answers, even to your advertising questions. People respond differently to messaging, so it's hard to know exactly what will resonate with your target market. You will probably be surprised which messages resonate and which fall on deaf ears, especially when you start out.

Marketing strategy is no different than product development in that your approach should be market-driven. Experiment with different messaging and channels, and react to feedback. Listen to customers, and be on the lookout for ways to get better.

A/B testing is a great way to test your messaging. Select a channel—direct mail, for example—and send out two different ads. Be sure that you can easily tell which ad people responded to.

The trick to maximize your learning is to begin broadly. Don't start your tests with minor differences, like colors. Instead, experiment with drastically different messaging. Only when you discover what broadly resonates with customers does it make sense to narrow in on specifics.

Even if you have years of experience, it's impossible to know what messages and channels will resonate with your target market. Try your advertising twice, and see what sticks.

The Agile Startup

PERCEPTION IS REALITY

The universal thorn in a startup's side is a constant lack of resources. Startups simply don't have the resources to launch national advertising campaigns, lease the best retail space, or build robust technology. But you can't look like a fly-by-night operation, either. For people to give you their money, they have to trust you. **The name of the game in Startupland is to create the impression that you are an established, trustworthy company.** To be taken seriously, you have to look bigger than a couple of hackers in a garage.

There are many ways to do this. Ultimately, it depends on the nature of your startup, but there are a few tried-and-true tactics. A 1-800-number with an interactive menu has a "big company" feel. Even better, have a virtual assistant patch through your calls. Media mentions can also be an effective way to demonstrate social proof. Major media logos on your website are a great way to establish credibility. To a lesser extent, testimonials are a way to create trust. Written testimonials are okay, but videos of your ecstatic customers are even better.

Perception is reality. If you want customers to buy from you, make sure that you're perceived as a winner.

BE A GUERRILLA MARKETER

Guerrilla marketing is a catchall term used to describe unconventional marketing tactics. **Guerrilla marketing is a cost-effective way to be different and get the word out,** which is why a lot of entrepreneurs are guerrillas at heart. Advertising is expensive. To put it in perspective, a one-page ad in most mainstream magazines can cost over $60,000. Even if you could afford this, it's probably not the best way to invest your marketing budget. Instead, get creative and be different.

Guerrilla marketing tactics are great for any size company. To help determine feasibility, you might rent a mall kiosk over a weekend or set up a trade show booth to see if there's enough demand for your idea. Contests with fun, whacky prizes can be a great way to get people engaged. Even bigger companies can get in on the action. Red Bull's marketing strategy has a distinctly guerrilla feel to it. They create and promote insane stunts and events, and get worldwide media coverage for it.

The best part of being a guerrilla is how much fun you'll have. How can you not have fun throwing wild parties, putting on insane stunts, or pulling pranks that get national media attention? Just make sure you don't get too crazy—you probably haven't allocated any of your marketing budget to post bail.

The Agile Startup

THE SECRET TO WRITING COPY THAT SELLS

It's not easy to write killer copy. Whether you are writing for your website, packaging, or an advertising campaign, writing copy that sells can be unexpectedly challenging. Realize we're talking about copy *that sells*, not necessarily great copy. You might find that short, terse sentences sell much better than poetic, profound paragraphs.

The secret to writing copy that sells is to get inside the head of your ideal customer. Write from the customer's perspective. To do this, ask questions: What do they care about? What do they *not* care about? What causes them to buy? What inspires and frustrates them? Some marketers go so far as to create personas, which describe their ideal customers in excruciating detail.

Knowing how your target customers think and feel will allow you to view the buying decision from their perspective. You'll be able to understand why certain benefits resonate with customers more than others, and how to influence them more effectively. You will be able to properly frame your benefits and clearly articulate how you're different than the competition. See the world from your ideal customer's perspective to write copy that sells.

PROMISE...THEN OVERDELIVER

The way you communicate and interact with potential customers creates an unspoken promise. Whether it's through advertising, packaging, or customer service, your communications let customers know what to expect. Marketers call these expectations your *brand promise*, and every company makes a promise in one form or another. Understanding and intentionally communicating your promise is an important first step to creating your brand, differentiating your offering, and forging a strong relationship with customers.

Typically, a brand promise is communicated internally and experienced externally, but some companies also make their promises their taglines. While there's no single formula to a winning brand promise, make sure you at least convey who you are and what you stand for. Think about Ritz Carlton's "Ladies and gentlemen serving ladies and gentlemen," or FedEx's "When it absolutely, positively has to get there overnight." Keep it short and impactful, and avoid generic or meaningless wording.

Your brand promise must set you up for success in the long run, so don't make promises you can't keep. The best way to build brand equity is to overdeliver on your promise and surpass expectations.

YOUR BRAND TALKS

CHAPTER 6

Team

A startup's founding team is the number-one determining factor of a startup's success or failure. That's why investors look for great teams first and foremost. The people behind the curtain are so important because the startup will encounter dozens of roadblocks and potholes. When these setbacks happen, the founders make decisions that will determine the fate of the company. Good decisions will lead to forward progress, but a few bad decisions can doom the company.

This chapter will help you understand why you should probably wait to partner, how to put together a powerhouse founding team, and best practices to make partnerships work.

The Agile Startup

NOT SO FAST, PARTNER

It's understandable why people are quick to partner—the risk and likelihood of failure are so great that having someone by your side can provide tremendous moral support. But there are a lot of drawbacks to bringing on a partner immediately. **While your partner's skills might be perfect at the outset, what happens when you pivot and your company morphs into something completely different?** You'll be tied to someone ill suited for your company. Having a partner to brainstorm with might result in better solutions, but it can also cause a lot of friction and bad compromises. Early hires or partnerships often make or break a new business, so the importance of waiting is not to be underestimated.

One of the best ways to beat these challenges is to wait to partner. This doesn't mean that you'll never have a partner, but that you'll have some room to explore and experiment first. Then, when you're ready to bring someone on, you'll have a solid understanding of what you need to build a great company. The best part of waiting to partner is that you'll have to give up a fraction of the equity you would at the outset. Build first, then partner.

GET A PRE-NUP

Would you get married to a person you've spent only a few days with? It may sound like an insane weekend in Vegas, but startup founders do this all the time. Not realizing the commitment it takes—years, not months—founders are notorious for haphazardly jumping into partnerships. Just as you would hesitate to get married after a weekend, take your time when looking for a business partner. Find someone whose long-term interests and vision align closely with yours. And whether your new partner is a weekend fling or a lifelong devotion, get a pre-nup.

The startup world's version of a pre-nup is a contract between partners that specifies exactly how the company will operate—everything from what equity is owned by whom to the details of what happens if the founding team breaks up. Get a great startup lawyer to make sure your pre-nup includes all of the important issues. Use this contract to protect your interests, and those of the company. So many startup failures happen as a result of poor partnership planning. It might be awkward to talk about contingencies, but it could save your company down the road.

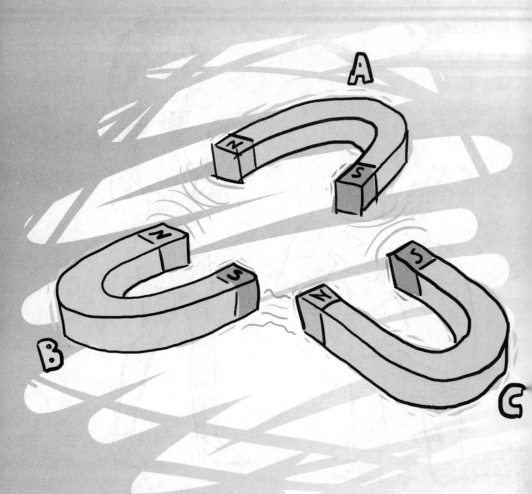

The Agile Startup

ABCS OF HIRING

Almost all startups have one of two kinds of teams: a strong team of "A" players, or a weak team with "B" and "C" players. Why this grouping? "A" people hire "A" and "A+" people. A's know their strengths, and have the confidence and fortitude to surround themselves with other high-quality individuals. On the other hand, B's hire C's because they hate to be upstaged and need to stroke their egos. As a company grows, like attracts like—**A's will attract A's, and B's will attract B's and C's. The stronger your team is, the easier it will be to get high-quality people on board.**

This ABC pattern is set extremely early in a company's lifecycle. Expectations are often set as soon as the first two or three hires. Because this is so important, always be aware of who your company is hiring. You hold the ultimate veto on any new hire, so interviewing every person yourself is a great idea. If you sense the quality of your people is going downhill, figure out the cause and correct it immediately. A teams win in the marketplace, so take your time and build a team you can be proud of.

YOUR STARTUP IS A BOAT

What are the three most important factors that determine the success or failure of a new company? Team, team, and—you guessed it—team. It's impossible to overstate the importance of the founding team.

Think of your startup as a boat. **Everyone on a boat has a job, and if they're not performing, then the boat will stall.** The story is the same with startups, but instead of stalling, your startup will crash and burn—nothing will sink a company faster than a bad founder or employee. Building a great team requires three key steps. First, get the right people on the boat. Second, get them in the right positions—different people have different strengths and weaknesses. Third, make sure the team has everything it needs to execute. The fate of any startup is determined by its people and their actions.

Just because someone on your team worked at Procter & Gamble doesn't mean that you have hired the necessary marketing experience. Make sure you plug the holes and cover key activities to keep your startup ship sailing.

THE BUILD/SELL TEAM

Peter Drucker, the father of modern management, famously said that **every business has two major functions: innovation and marketing** (see page 151). In other words, the purpose of your business is to build great products and find profitable customers. To generate meaningful and sustainable revenue, your company needs to innovate rapidly and market effectively. These are essential ingredients of successful startups, so the best teams are those with build/sell experience in spades. For evidence of this, look no further than the hacker/hustler founding teams that many seed stage investors *require* to invest. The hacker builds and the hustler sells. Many early investors won't even consider you for an investment unless you have a build/sell team in place.

When establishing your initial team, or evaluating potential team members, focus on build/sell capabilities. Other skills are on the periphery, and won't directly contribute to your startup's success. Make sure new hires understand their roles, and then stand aside and let them execute. If you do hire someone who can build or sell, your runway will be that much longer when they start producing. If not, you'll actually shorten your runway, making it that much harder to get off the ground.

MAKE SURE YOU'RE ALIGNED

Starting a business is a long-term commitment, so you need to make sure that you and your partners will be aligned well into the future. **It's crucial that all founders' visions for the future, both near-term and long-term, are similar.** If you want to build a $100 million business, but your partner would be perfectly happy making $100,000, you will run into problems. Sometime in the future, your partner will want to slow things down, and take some money off the table. Of course, this will be about the same time that you'll want to expand and grow. Situations like these don't end well, and can easily end your partnership.

The key is to set expectations from the beginning. Have open and candid conversations about your vision for the company, the product roadmap, and what you want personally out of life. Lay it all out, and make sure that your future selves are as compatible as your current selves. If there are red flags, don't ignore them and hope for the best. As uncomfortable as it may be, it's much better to resolve issues sooner rather than later, when the stakes are a lot higher.

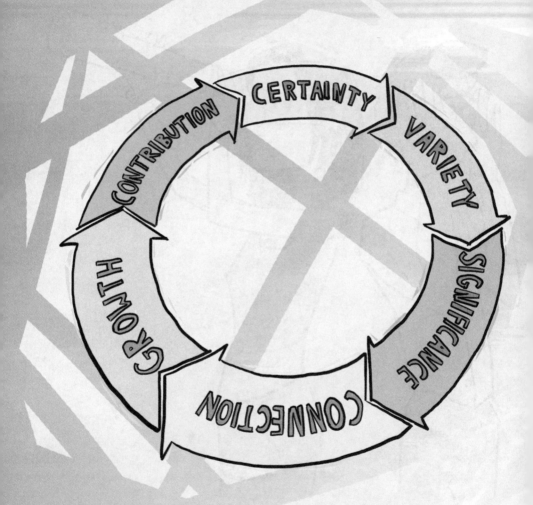

HOW TO GET THE BEST PEOPLE

Getting top talent can require paying the highest salaries, but not always. Stock options are an obvious incentive to keep your employees invested in your company's success. But salary and stock options are extrinsic motivators that will only get you so far.

Often, the best motivation doesn't come from outside rewards, it comes from within. Everybody has six basic human needs in life: certainty, variety, significance, connection, growth, and contribution. Find out which of the needs excite your prospective hire, and then show how the job directly links to those needs. You see this done all the time with social startups, which link their companies to some greater good, such as a BHAG (big, hairy, audacious goal) or an emotional social issue.

Beyond extrinsic and intrinsic motivators, there are a lot of startup perks that make you more attractive than corporate America, such as a flexible schedule, constant challenge and variety, and the feeling of accomplishment.

Look for people who thrive in the challenging startup environment, understand their motivations, and link their jobs to those motivators. You'll be amazed at what you can pull off.

FIRE YOURSELF

Different modes of leadership are required to transition your company from inception to maturity. Broadly, you can split a company's lifecycle into two phases—search and growth. At inception, a visionary entrepreneur is needed, with all the expected characteristics: bold, risk-taking, thrives on uncertainty, action-oriented, short attention span, and so on. These characteristics, for better or worse, are what allow a company to discover a repeatable and sustainable way to make a profit.

However, the game changes drastically after you nail your business model. Once this happens, the business enters a growth phase, which requires a manager instead of an entrepreneur. While the entrepreneur searches, the manager refines and streamlines. The growth mode is much more methodical, process oriented, and predictable. The typical entrepreneur usually scores negatively in all of these areas, and can actually hurt the company's prospects.

Rare is the founder who can lead effectively in both entrepreneur and manager modes. They call for completely different skills and temperaments. And the stakes are high—transitional mistakes are usually company killers. Consequently, many experienced founders would rather hand over the reins to a professional management team and start over again with a new company. Isn't that the fun part anyway?

The Agile Startup

YOU ARE NOT SCALABLE

When you first started out, you did everything yourself. You designed the brochures, you called on customers, and you responded to every e-mail. Heck, you probably even built the website yourself. But in your quest to build a scalable startup you must realize that *you* are not scalable. **There are only so many hours in the day, and you cannot have your finger in every pie as the company grows.** To continue to do everything yourself is not only impossible, it's ridiculous. More than just annoying your team, your reluctance to delegate will be a major bottleneck to your company's continued growth.

Working with others requires trust and humility. You have to trust your team with greater responsibilities, and you have to be humble enough to see that others can execute as well as you can. Your time is better spent on things that only you can do—strategy, vision, partnerships, and morale.

Most entrepreneurs have trouble letting go of the details, so this might be hard for you. Think of yourself as a movie producer. Your purpose is not to execute every detail of the project, but to get the right people in place, who can execute your grand vision. Show your team the vision, and then help them execute.

MESS WITH THE VEST, DIE LIKE THE REST

Vesting is a way to make people earn their equity over time. Instead of giving 100 percent of an equity grant up front, vesting allows you to award it over time. With a four-year vest, which is the usual amount of time to vest, equity would not be awarded in full until after four years have passed.

You can choose to award the prorated equity in monthly or yearly installments (known as *cliffs*). After 18 months, a four-year vest of 10 percent with a monthly cliff results in 3.75 percent equity earned (18 months passed/48 month vest × 10 percent equity grant). With an annual cliff, the same 18-month time period results in only 2.5 percent earned, since the second year hasn't yet been reached (1/4 × 10 percent).

Vesting creates a strong incentive for your employees and partners to stick around. It protects you if they decide to leave early, since they get to keep only the equity that they've earned. Everyone in the company with equity should be subject to a vest, especially cofounders. Without a vest, your 50 percent partner can leave after a few months and keep all 50 percent.

DELEGATE, DON'T ABDICATE

The temptation of every overworked entrepreneur is to hand off responsibilities as quickly as possible. **Don't delegate duties until you've done the job yourself first.** To do otherwise is to abdicate, not delegate. Whether it's a lack of time or a low confidence, abdicating responsibility is irresponsible. Even if you're a terrible salesperson, try to drum up a few sales before hiring anyone else to take over.

Proper delegation is essential. First and foremost, you'll learn critical information by doing the job yourself. By going on a few sales calls, for example, you might realize that a core feature of your product completely missed the mark. Good luck discovering this insight through a game of telephone with your new salesperson, who barely knows the product, doesn't understand customers' needs, and probably doesn't care about your company's long-term success.

More than feedback, you need to know what it takes to get the job done. By doing it yourself first, you'll know what to look for when hiring. Also, you will be able to tell when the person you just hired is cutting corners or trying to pull a fast one on you.

Don't abdicate. Do the job yourself first, and then delegate.

FORM AN ADVISORY BOARD

You need an advisory board to hold you accountable and challenge you. Forming a board actually isn't that difficult once you know how they're structured. **Your goal should be to have four or five accomplished business people on your board, who have a mix of startup or industry experience.** Create a short list of potential advisors, and then get to know each person over a few meals. Test the waters and probe to see if their experience would be valuable to your company, given its long-term direction. You know you've got a good fit when they get excited about your business and the prospect of getting involved.

Once you have advisors on the hook, it's time to reel them in. Do this by putting some equity on the line. Normally, an advisor gets 0.5 to 1.0 percent in exchange for advising you over a set period of time, usually two years. In exchange for the equity, they agree to meet at least once a month for an hour. In these meetings, usually conference calls with your entire board, explain your most pressing issues. After you explain the situation, stop talking and let your advisors earn their equity. If you've succeeded in putting together the right advisory board, the advice you get should be pure gold.

WHO'S THE BOSS?

When it comes to partnering with someone else, **the only time a 50/50 equity split makes sense is when you can't do it without the other guy.** If this isn't the case, the person who's bringing more to the table should get more equity. Everything feels equal in a 50/50 startup, which can handicap you because it's harder to make decisions. The company needs a boss to call the shots and keep things moving forward quickly. This is usually the person who owns more equity in the company.

There are a few ways to determine who should get more equity, but more is usually given to the person who came up with the idea, who has put in more time, and who brings more value to the table. If you're pursuing a biotech solution, and your partner invented the technology over the last five years, it probably makes sense that she would be the majority owner. If you plan to quit your job and work on this full-time, while your partner can only commit 10 hours a week, you should get most of the equity. Give this a lot of time and attention—misallocating equity because no one wanted to broach the topic can lead to resentment that festers over time. It's infinitely better to figure it out at the beginning.

THE RIGHT PARTNER FORMULA

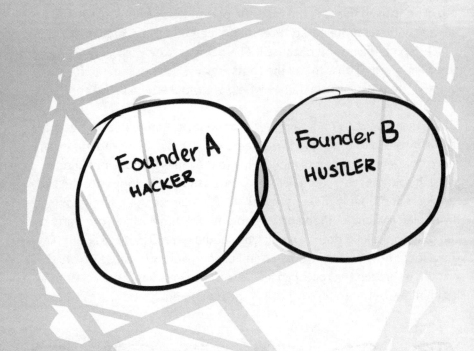

HIRE SLOW, FIRE FAST

SHARING A SUBMARINE

Before you partner with anyone, ask yourself, **"Would I share a submarine with this person?"** Given the long and hard hours you will spend together, this isn't much of a stretch. If this is impossible to imagine, proceed with caution.

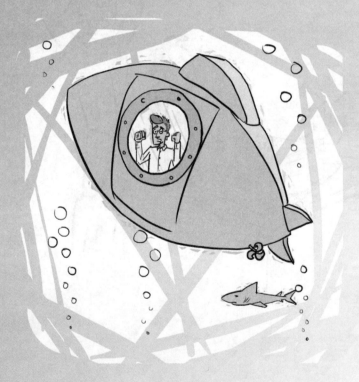

CHAPTER 7

Pitching Your Startup

As an entrepreneur, you're a salesperson above all else. You have to pitch constantly to potential customers, partners, investors, suppliers, and even family members. If you can't pitch, then you can't close deals, which means you'll have a heck of a time succeeding. There's an art to pitching in a way that gets people excited and interested. In this chapter, you'll learn important tactics, such as why it's important to have two versions of your pitch, a surprisingly simple way to figure out if your pitch is working, and how to get your audience to understand your business idea in less than three seconds. Put these practices into place to wow your audience at any stage of the game.

GET YOUR STORY STRAIGHT

There are four kinds of pitches that you should master to wow your audience in any situation: the tagline, one-liner, elevator pitch, and full presentation.

A tagline is your motto, or a catchy, public-facing phrase that you use to get attention and quickly convey what your company or product is about. Think "Just Do It" from Nike.

A one-liner is exactly what it sounds like—a one-sentence summary of your business. Keep it clear, short, and impactful. Avoid the temptation to throw in fancy (and confusing) words. Tease your audience with exciting highlights, such as deals done, celebrities involved, paying customers, and so on. If you've phrased it properly, your one-liner will prompt intrigue and questions.

An elevator pitch is a 30- to 60-second summary of your business. You have at most a minute, so don't try to cover every aspect your business. Hit the highlights, and leave your audience begging for more.

Finally, you must master a full presentation of your business. These types of presentations are typically 10 to 15 minutes long, and include some kind of presentation materials. This pitch is usually given to an investment committee, and Q&A typically follows.

Usually, the best way to pitch is to severely limit what you say, and maximize the amount of time for dialogue and questions. Tell your audience what you're about, and then let them dig into what's most interesting to them.

GET TO THE NEXT STEP

Any time you pitch, first figure out what you want to accomplish. Your intended outcomes will affect what you say and how you say it. When talking to an investor at a networking event, for example, many entrepreneurs make the mistake of diving into their full presentations. They lose sight of the fact that the appropriate outcome at an event should be to get a meeting, not cash a check.

Whether you are pitching your one-liner or your full-blown presentation, your goal is usually pretty simple—get to the next step. When formally pitching an investor, for example, your goal is to pass the first screen and move forward in their evaluation process. It's unheard of to get a check on the spot, so don't try to get one. When you run into a potential customer at a networking event, pitch in a way to get a meeting, not a purchase order.

Focus on your next steps, and do only what's necessary to get there. Don't inundate your listeners with pointless detail that causes them to tune out of the conversation. Be considerate of the situation, and get to the point quickly. Know what comes next, and ask for it.

HALF AS LONG IS TWICE AS GOOD

An audience rarely likes to listen as much as you like to talk, especially when it comes to your startup. Empathize with your audience, and **make your presentation impactful and interesting** *for them.* The best way to do this is to shorten your presentation and spend your time talking about what your audience wants to hear. When it comes to the time you present, half as long is twice as good, and vice versa.

The easiest way to understand what your audience wants to hear is to ask. Don't tell investors what you think they want to hear. Give them the elevator pitch and ask them what they want to know. Get through your materials and onto Q&A as quickly as possible. Focus on what matters to them.

When revising your presentation, cut out as much as you possibly can. And then cut some more. Send it to your co-founder or advisor and ask what you can get rid of. Less is more, so become a minimalist. The less you talk, the more time for questions and dialogue, which is where you learn what matters anyway.

Minimize the amount of time you spend talking—your audience will thank you for it.

FIRST RULE OF ELEVATOR PITCHES

A great elevator pitch is more sizzle than steak. While there's no right formula for an elevator pitch, the best usually has these elements: offering, pain point, market data, traction, and call to action. To be able to follow the entire pitch, **the listener should perfectly understand your offering (product/service) at the outset.** Once your offering is understood, highlight the pain you solve. This is usually best told in the form of a story or use case. Sprinkle in exciting data and trends about the market that hint that this could be a huge opportunity. Then, move on to cover any interesting traction you've gotten so far. Finally, close with a call to action.

While there's no right time limit for an elevator pitch, the norm is 30 to 60 seconds. If it's any longer, you run the risk of boring your listeners. And the first rule of elevator pitches is to never bore your listeners.

Your elevator pitch is the most versatile presentation tool in your arsenal. You should know it so well that you could recite it backwards. It's powerful because it can be used in so many situations. Even in a full 15-minute presentation, for example, many founders open with their elevator pitch to get the audience excited and convey the big picture.

GET USED TO REJECTION

G enerating sales is one of your top jobs as an entrepreneur. Build something, pitch it, sell it, and repeat. The process is easy to understand, but hard to execute. Especially early on, for every "yes," you will hear "no" dozens (or hundreds) of times. Colonel Sanders got rejected 1,001 times before he signed his first customer. Not everyone is an early adopter, and most people have trouble trusting a brand new company.

If you want to start a company, get used to constantly hearing "no." Some days, it will feel like the world wants to hold you back. Because of this, the people who build companies are among the toughest around. They have to be—they wade through miles of rejection for that one redeeming and glorious customer.

There are two ways to look at rejection—you can take it personally or use it to make your pitch stronger. **Great entrepreneurs love to hear "no," because every rejection teaches them something.** Do the same, and keep your sanity by turning sales into a game. See how many rejections it takes to get to a sale. Then try to beat that the next time around. Use rejection to build better products and a stronger company.

USE THE USE CASE

A use case is a great way to help your audience understand how your product or service will be used by your customers. The use case is a story that showcases the pain you're solving, and how an average customer would *use* your solution. The miracle of a use case is that it allows your listener to understand, with great clarity, the problem you target and the benefit of your solution. It takes a nebulous, theoretical concept and makes it concrete and tangible. **Through the use case, your offering becomes an imaginable solution to a definite problem or need.** For example, if you are pitching a radical new method that helps to manage emphysema, don't lose your audience by diving into hardcore science. Instead, explain how the large oxygen bottles that patients have to lug around are frustrating and embarrassing. Then highlight how your solution will markedly improve the lives of those living with the disease.

There will be times when, no matter how detailed your explanations, your audience simply won't understand. A use case is a great way to hammer home your value, and help your audience appreciate why what you're doing is so important.

MAKE IT STICK

As advertising execs know better than anyone, repetition is the key to building brand awareness. The same is true when you present. A complicated, multi-faceted message won't stick. **To keep your takeaways from getting lost in the mix, limit yourself to a maximum of three key messages.** Relate all aspects of your presentation to at least one of the messages, and reiterate the key takeaways often. One way to do this is, as the expression goes, to tell them what you are going to tell them, tell them, and then tell them what you told them.

Imagine this: You're about to give your presentation when an investor tells you that she'll fund your round under one condition—three people, independently polled, must be able to tell her all three of your key messages.

Before your next presentation, ask what two or three messages you want the audience to take away from your presentation. Chances are, about the same time that you start to feel like an idiot from repeating yourself so many times, the message will start to get through.

NAME IT AND FRAME IT

How can you convey your idea in three seconds or less? One tried-and-true way is to **relate your business to a concept or company that is already well-known.** Rather than trying to explain that you sell coupons for a limited time at deep discounts for extreme sports and outdoor adventures, you can simply say you're the "Groupon of extreme sports." Instead of trying to explain that you're building a directory of all nonprofit organizations that volunteers can use to find, rate, and review nonprofits, you can simply say that you are "Yelp for nonprofits." If your comparison is a good one, it will take a few seconds for your audience to understand what you do.

There are a few formats you can use to frame your concept properly. You can say "X for Y," where X is the comparable company and Y is the new category or space. Alternatively, you can say "X meets Y," where you are combining services of both X and Y companies. To elaborate, you can say "X for Y," but with Z, where Z is your special sauce.

As effective as this tactic can be, it can also go horribly wrong. Choose your comparison carefully, and pay attention to whether it helps or hurts your cause. If you find yourself failing, then reframe and try again, or don't frame it at all. It won't work for every company.

FIND THE HOT BUTTONS

Long gone are the hard-sell days of scripted, uninterrupted presentations. Face-to-face selling today requires a consultative approach. Rather than steamrolling your audience, you need to probe in order to uncover needs. Salespeople call these needs or problems *hot buttons*. On a sales call, your mission is to find the hot buttons, and then demonstrate how your product fixes them. For example, let's say that your plan is to present five problems that your product addresses. In probing, you discover that only one of the five areas is a hot button. Realizing this, focus all of your efforts on the hot button and forget the other four talking points. Above all, **engage with your audience, understand what motivates them, and respond to those hot buttons.**

This agile approach to presentations works with all kinds of audiences, even investors. In the meeting, rather than barreling through your pitch, pause frequently and ask probing questions. Find the investors' hot buttons, and then leverage this information to lead them to the conclusion that your company belongs in their portfolio.

FAKE IT 'TIL YOU MAKE IT

As an entrepreneur, you will be out of your element often. At the beginning, when you have to do everything yourself, you will always feel like you're behind the eight ball. You will have to learn how to do so many things along the way—talk to customers, build technology, handle suppliers, conform to industry norms, manufacture your products, and everything in-between. **A hallmark of the serial entrepreneur is the ability to exude confidence, even in moments of extreme uncertainty.** Often, successful entrepreneurs' favorite war stories are about these moments of extreme uncertainty when a bluff paid off. Take risks and be bold, but don't make promises you can't keep—you won't get a second chance.

Acting the part is especially important when pitching your startup to investors or prospective employees. For example, you might be asked to predict where the market is going over the next two years, when you might not feel comfortable predicting what will happen in the next two weeks. It's important to reassure your audience, and convince them that you have the special insight required to build a winner. Be certain about what you don't know, and fake it 'til you make it.

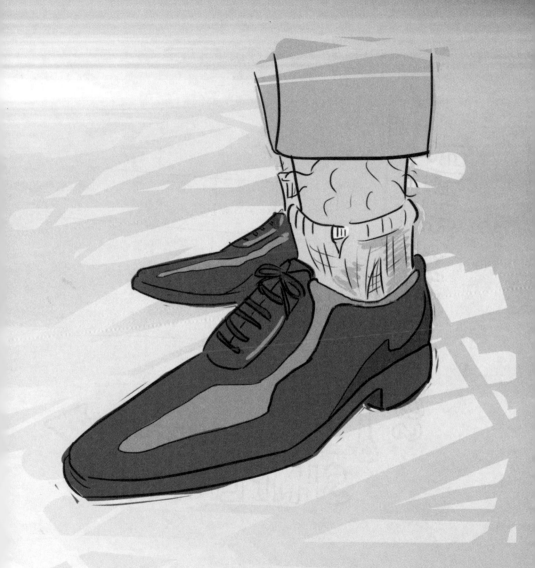

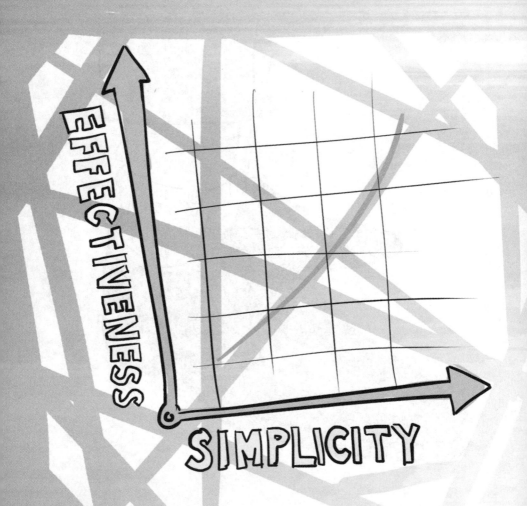

The Agile Startup

BE SIMPLE, NOT SIMPLISTIC

Why do we always overcomplicate things? Especially when it comes to presentations, big words and dazzling animations are more likely to confuse and distract your audience than gain their confidence. Follow the K.I.S.S. rule—keep it simple, stupid. As Leonardo da Vinci said, "Simplicity is the ultimate sophistication." Leave the esoteric, sophisticated language to academics and keep your audience engaged. In business, **it's a thousand times better to be simple and understood than complex and confusing.** That's why top businesspeople—Warren Buffett, Steve Jobs, and Bill Gates, among others—have a knack for taking complex issues and explaining them in a way that even a fifth grader can understand. An audience's attention span is notoriously short, so don't make them try to figure out what you're saying. Simplify and make sure you're understood.

Simplicity is the objective, but don't just dumb it down. The difference between dumbing it down and distilling complexity into simplicity is like night and day. You get to simplicity through complexity. Once you have your arms wrapped around the issues, simplify. Less is more. Focus on the core ideas. Use graphics instead of text, and avoid slideshow animations. Tell stories, employ use cases, and use everyday language.

DON'T BURY THE LEAD

Journalists use the phrase "bury the lead" when they don't hook the reader in the first line with the most interesting fact or insight. The same is true for your pitch—don't bury the lead. **The first 30 seconds of your presentation is your chance to hook the audience.** The way you handle the opening will set you up for a smashing success or a painful flop. You've already won half the battle if you can immediately grab the audience's attention.

There are many ways to make your opening attention-getting and memorable, but a story is the most common. To do this effectively, tell an emotionally charged story about your history, your mission, or your product. Your story should make the audience say either "wow" or "me too." Stun them with your story of struggle and triumph that pulls at their heartstrings, blow them away with your technology, or get them to relate to the frustrating pain that you solve.

Whatever you decide to do, don't bury the lead. Make your opening exciting, captivating, and memorable.

BACK OF A BUSINESS CARD

You should be able to summarize your business on the back of a business card.

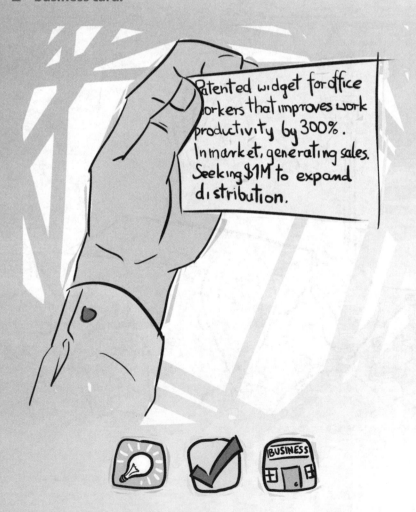

CHAPTER 8

Investors

Investors are an indispensable part of the startup landscape. Especially when it comes to technology companies, investors provide the fuel entrepreneurs need to turn their small companies into national brands. Without investors, growth can be painfully slow, if not impossible.

While investors can be a blessing, they can also be a curse. Set your company up for success by following the investor strategies in this chapter. In it, you'll learn the right timing for an investment, how to find the perfect investor, and how to determine if you even need one in the first place.

YOU ARE THE FIRST INVESTOR

Even if you're bootstrapping, you always have an investor. You are your business's first and most important investor. **And you invest something much more important than cash—*your life*.** You put everything on the line to attempt a treacherous mountain climb, upon a crumbling path that is littered with the tombstones of failed startups. If you give anything less, you might as well quit now. You'll never make it halfheartedly.

Since you're the first investor, you must evaluate your business as an investor would. Is the industry good? Is the market receptive to new entrants? Can I make enough money to be happy in the long run? Is the reward worth the risk? Is the go-to-market plan realistic or a pipe dream? Pretend that an entrepreneur trying to raise money pitched you *your* company. Would you invest 20 percent of your net worth? Be honest with yourself! This is one of the hardest things for entrepreneurs to do, but it's also one of the most important.

If you come to the difficult conclusion that you wouldn't invest, what holds you back? Can you fix or mitigate the issue? If you can't justify investing 20 percent of your net worth, how can you justify investing your life? Don't rush into a business that isn't right for you. Take your time, and wait for the right idea. It will come.

GOT TRACTION?

Investors care most about traction, especially when it comes to valuations. You'll probably deal with investors who don't know you personally, so they have to make educated guesses about your philosophy and work ethic. **Traction shows them that your business is more than an idea, and that you're more than another "wantrapreneur."**

There are many ways to show traction, but investors care most about customers and revenue. Cash is king. Land your first customer before your big pitch, and the tone of the conversation will change from one of skepticism about you and your idea, to enthusiasm and respect. When you have revenue, the investors' main concern changes from "Is this a real business?" to "How scalable is it?"

There are many other ways to show traction: obtain letters of intent, build an e-mail list, get notable people in the industry to join your board or team, build a prototype, file for a trademark or patent, or get a deal with a strategic partner.

Investors care about traction so much because it's a good indicator of progress. The more traction you have, the easier it is to believe that you're the team that will make it happen.

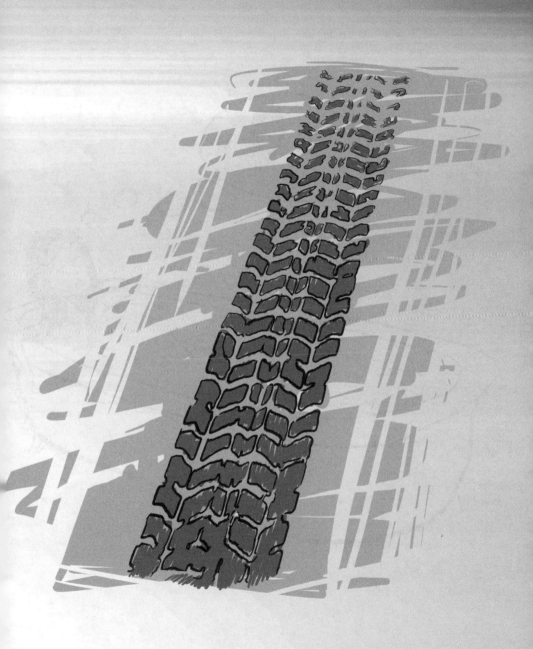

PASSIONATE OBSESSED

Investors need to know that you're committed to building a blockbuster business with every fiber of your being. They want your business on your mind 24 hours a day, seven days a week. It's a good sign to investors if you even dream about your business. In short, investors look for entrepreneurs who are ~~passionate~~ obsessed with their businesses.

Anything less is usually a deal-breaking red flag for investors. Why would they bet on you if you won't bet on yourself? There are many ways to demonstrate your obsession, but three really count in an investor's mind. First, you can't build a blockbuster business in your spare time, so you should quit your job if you can. Second, don't try to start two or three businesses at the same time, spend all of your time building this one. Third, have some skin in the game by investing your own capital. The dollar amount isn't as important as the percentage of your net worth. You should invest (or be prepared to invest) a significant percentage of your net worth.

Anything less than all-out obsession makes it too easy for you to walk away. Investors know that obsession is what keeps your startup ship sailing through even the worst storms, which you'll inevitably face.

PIGS GET SLAUGHTERED

Whether it's with investors, partners, or employees, don't be too greedy with your equity. Hoarding equity might mean that you retain ownership of your company, but owning all of the equity of a dying or stagnating business is worthless. **One hundred percent of nothing is nothing.** Selling equity to investors gives you the capital, mentorship, and connections you need to quickly scale. Paying employees partly in equity creates an ownership mentality, which makes them dedicated to the long-term success of your business. Giving strategic partners the option to buy a piece of your company can cause them to go to extremes to help you succeed.

Smart entrepreneurs know how to use equity to align incentives and get people excited about their businesses. Think of your equity as another tool in your arsenal, and welcome opportunities to use it strategically. After all, a small piece of a big pie can be worth a lot more than 100 percent of nothing. Have a strong sense of your company's worth, but don't be a pig—pigs get slaughtered.

The Agile Startup

INVESTORS ARE NOT CREATED EQUAL

Contrary to popular belief, most investors are specialists and invest only in their areas of expertise. Through specialization, they're able to gain an advantage over fellow investors and identify promising investment opportunities. All but the biggest investors focus on particular domains. Many new founders looking to raise money for their startup will pitch to any investor who will listen. While most investors will take a meeting, few are actually eligible to invest. **Fundraising is basically a full-time job, so you have to be selective, and focus your efforts where you're most likely to succeed.** Your time is best spent with investors who are active in your space and have capital to invest (many funds are already fully committed).

Do your homework to make sure that you're not spinning your wheels. There are a number of ways to figure out an investor's specialties. Most investors announce their areas of interest on their website. If it's not clear, you can always ask. The next best method is to look at their portfolio companies. If they have companies in their portfolio in your space, you're off to a good start. You can also look at the backgrounds and areas of expertise of the people who run the firm. Finally, you can also track down investors by looking at other funded companies in your space.

While it may feel great to get a meeting with an investor, getting a check is really what counts.

DO YOU WANT TO BE RICH OR BE KING?

This is a favorite closing line that venture capitalists use to seal a deal. When you're starting out, you own 100 percent of the company, which means you call all of the shots. You are the king. However, most companies eventually hit a growth plateau that requires capital to break through. It is at this point you have to decide whether you want to be king or be rich. The implication, of course, is that by taking an investor's money, you'll become rich. While there may be strong arguments for fueling growth through outside capital, it's not without its disadvantages. Investors' terms can be quite onerous, and compel you to do things that you wouldn't otherwise do. Examples of the interests of investors and entrepreneurs diverging abound, and usually to the entrepreneurs' disadvantage.

There's no right answer—yours will depend entirely on what kind of business and lifestyle you want to create. Many entrepreneurs get mesmerized with the idea of building a $100 million company, and believe the only way forward is to take an investor's money. While this may be true, there's nothing wrong with growing organically. Ultimately, your happiness should determine your answer—would you be happier being rich or being the king?

WHEN NO LEADS TO YES

Entrepreneurs and investors look at the world fundamentally differently. **Entrepreneurs are always looking for ways to say "yes," while investors look for any excuse to say "no."** They'll take the first opportunity you give them to reject your business as flawed, and move onto the next investment opportunity. This is the nature of the game, so your job is not to give an investor a reason to say "no." By avoiding "no," eventually you'll get to "yes."

Make sure you don't make one of these common mistakes that will ruin your chances:

- Not investing yourself, or asking friends or family to invest. If you don't have any skin in the game, why should an investor?
- Viral marketing plan. If your customer acquisition strategy is to "go viral," you're dead in the water. You might as well call it quits.
- A weak or nonexistent advisory team. If you can't get any heavyweights on your advisory team, the investor will doubt that your startup's concept or technology is very interesting.

If you can't check all of these boxes, make sure you have solid reasons why.

THE TRAIN IS LEAVING THE STATION

To get investors excited about your business, you have to convey a sense of unstoppable momentum. You have to **give the impression that your startup train is leaving the station with or without them.** Investors are notorious for dragging their feet, and too many idle investors are a recipe for fundraising disaster.

Creating this feeling is much more an art than a science. Landing an investor is like trying to get a first date: You have to look like a winner, move quickly, be in high demand, and not look too desperate. Send out e-mail updates at regular intervals with evidence of your impending success. An end date on which the round officially closes is a good way to instill a sense of urgency in your investors. But this is also a gamble, because if you don't have all of the money committed by then, you'll have to extend the deadline, which is a negative signal.

The tricky thing is that all of this needs to happen quickly—in weeks, not months—to build a sense of urgency. Moving swiftly creates a fever pitch, and causes investors go to extremes to jump on board. To do this, you'll need to start laying the groundwork many months in advance. Plan carefully, and start communicating with investors early.

CALLING ALL ANGELS

Angel investors, or wealthy individuals who invest their own money, are typically a company's first source of financing. They invest for a variety of reasons, but most of the time it's because they want to give back and help up-and-coming entrepreneurs. Altruism aside, they also want a return on their investment. Because they want to help, they'll probably be active in your company's day-to-day operations. There are three types of angel investors, and you should pursue them in the following order:

1. Serial entrepreneur, startup expert
2. Industry veteran, expert in your market
3. Unsophisticated, with little business experience

Ideally, your investor is both (1) and (2)—a serial entrepreneur with a lot of industry experience. An angel with a lot of startup experience will know how to roll with the startup punches, so he or she will understand when things go wrong. If you can't find a serial entrepreneur, the next best thing is someone who understands the industry pitfalls, and has a robust network that you can call on for help. Unsophisticated angels who have never built a business before or don't understand business, can be more trouble than they're worth. Other than the money, they add little value. It's best to avoid these kinds of investors.

Your angel investors will be hands-on in your business, so make sure it's a good long-term fit.

THE LEMMINGS NEED A LEADER

Investors are often compared to lemmings, and for good reason. Lemmings move together in groups, and blindly follow each other. **Like lemmings, investors feel most comfortable in packs and follow other investors.** To raise capital from multiple investors, you need to find a leader among the lemmings. Otherwise, you'll have a lot of conversations, and maybe even get a few soft commitments, but no one will write a check. The trouble is that most investors won't tell you "no" outright, so you need a way to tell if they're serious. If you find yourself in this situation, focus your efforts on securing a lead investor who will show the other lemmings the way. A lead investor will offer you terms that you can take to other investors. You can take the term sheet to the followers and say, "Here's the deal—take it or leave it." Without a lead, you'll feel like you're spinning your wheels.

If you can't get an investor to step up and take the lead, try sweetening the deal for them by offering extra incentives such as warrant coverage or bonus stock.

The Agile Startup

DON'T EXPECT TO HEAR "NO"

Most investors suffer from a disease—the fear of missing out (FOMO). This disease heavily influences how entrepreneurs are treated, especially those hoping for an investment decision. Most business deals conclude with a definitive "yes" or "no." Not so with FOMO, which has struck "no" from most investors' vocabularies. They simply can't say it because they don't want to miss out on what could be a great investment. **By not giving you a definitive "no," investors leave the door open if they want to walk through it later.** Since you'll rarely hear "no" outright, FOMO causes a lot of false hope and wasted energy.

Many entrepreneurs think, "They haven't said 'no' and they keep meeting with us, so they must still be interested, right?" Wrong. They won't reject you because you might either: (1) get a lot of traction or (2) get other big-name investors interested. If either happens, they still have the option to invest.

Fundraising is so time-consuming that it can suck the life out of you, so try to determine as early as possible who is stringing you along and who is actually serious. Don't waste your time on FOMO investors—you've got a business to build.

SAVE THE BEST FOR LAST

It will take hundreds of hours of practice and dozens of iterations to perfect your pitch. You'll discover that things you thought were straightforward are too complicated to explain in one meeting. In the beginning, you'll be all over the place as you try to get through all of your material. Most importantly, when you first start pitching, you won't have a strong sense of what investors will care about.

The only way to improve and get a sense of investors' concerns is to pitch to real investors. The more you pitch, the better you'll get and the more you'll learn. As a result, save your best investor pitches for last. **Start with your least favorite investors and work to improve your pitch and get an investor's perspective.** Learn what they're most concerned about, how they evaluate your opportunity, and what gets them excited. When you're ready, blow away your top choice investors with a pitch that exudes confidence, addresses their concerns in advance, and showcases your company as a great investment opportunity.

GET TO YOUR NEXT MILESTONE

Investors want to know specifically what you plan to spend their money on. Wantrapreneurs have vague and confused answers that will leave them dead in the water. Experienced entrepreneurs have detailed and logical answers that convey the confidence that investors need to see.

To determine how much money you should raise, you have to figure out how much money you need to get to your next significant milestone. Getting to the next milestone is important because achieving the milestone will set you up to raise additional funds down the road, if necessary. If you only get halfway to a milestone without much to show for the last round of funding, investors will perceive you as a risk and you'll take a hit on your valuation (if you get any interest, of course).

After you've determined how much you need to hit your next milestone, add in a six-month buffer by multiplying your post-investment monthly burn rate by six. Things always cost more and take longer than expected, so you need a buffer to protect yourself. Add these two numbers together—the milestone cost and the buffer—to figure out about how much money you need to raise.

On average, the number of months of operations funded is usually around 18 to 24 months.

FUEL TO THE FIRE

To understand the differences between investors and entrepreneurs, think of your startup as a fire. It is the entrepreneur who decides to build a fire, gets the right resources in place by collecting kindling and firewood, and provides the initial spark. Up until this point, investors are only spectators who watch you run around frantically to get the fire started, and occasionally lob opinions your way. **It's only when you have the fire burning, and there's potential to turn it into something much bigger, that an investor will jump in to help.** Even when investors get involved, their main function is simply to add fuel to the fire. By injecting additional capital, they can help you grow the fire faster and burn stronger.

Realizing that an investor's main function is simply to add fuel to the fire, you'll better understand their motivations and desires. You'll avoid making mistakes like asking for an investment when you're not ready, or hoping to get more than capital.

The Agile Startup

A DEMO IS WORTH 1,000 WORDS

With investors, a prototype or demo is worth 1,000 words—other than customers and revenue, nothing makes a stronger initial impression. People are visual, so **a prototype allows your audience to grasp your business immediately.** This is a huge advantage, because investors are notoriously impatient with entrepreneurs, especially when they're pitching.

However, the demo advantage goes much deeper than conveying an idea. It says things for you that you can't easily say. Through a demo, your audience will get a sense of your approach and your vision. The more impressive it is, the more points you'll get on your credibility in product development and user experience.

Most importantly, a demo or prototype establishes that you're a doer, not a dreamer. It proves that you get things done. When you're unknown to a prospective investor, the main thing he's trying to figure out is whether you've got what it takes to build the business. A demo of your prototype is a big step in the right direction.

Besides, with prototypes being so quick and easy to build these days, if you're really serious about your business why wouldn't you start building?

MONEY ONLY BUYS TIME

A lot of entrepreneurs mistakenly equate fundraising with progress. They talk about raising a round as if they just hit a major business milestone. You can tell that an entrepreneur has fallen into this trap when parties are thrown after closing a round. Or, when asked about the company, the entrepreneur brags about his latest investors. This is the wrong way to look at it. Getting a new investor is not a milestone, and additional capital does not guarantee that your company will be successful. **Money only buys you more time to succeed or fail.** Sure, the cash is important. The number-one reason businesses fail is that they are undercapitalized. But look at the long, distinguished line of startup tombstones that have raised tens or hundreds of millions of dollars and still flopped. Capital only gives you time to make your business model work or to postpone your death. It's what you do with the money that counts.

The Agile Startup

IF YOU WANT MONEY, ASK FOR ADVICE

There's an old adage when it comes to investors: "If you want money, ask for advice. If you want advice, ask for money." **The best way to set your company up for fundraising success is to build relationships with investors over time.** And the best way to build relationships is to ask for advice.

Your investor bonding formula should follow this sequence: (1) update the investor about your business, (2) ask for advice on key strategic decisions, (3) declare your intention to do something the investor recommends, (4) go do it, (5) report your achievement, and (6) meet and repeat. The third and fourth steps—declare and do—are the most important. When it comes to delivering on your promises, make sure that you underpromise and overdeliver. By outperforming expectations, you'll build a reputation for making things happen. Ideally, over time, your momentum will make your mentor/investors excited to join the party.

The more time an investor has to get to know you and understand your business, the better your chances when asking for money. While there's no right time to meet an investor, the wrong time is at your first pitch. Start early and ask for advice.

THE INVESTOR TRIAD

Sophisticated investors evaluate three central areas of a potential investment: the team, the market, and the product. Different investors weight the three sides of the triad differently, but all three are vital to building a scalable, thriving startup.

The team is almost universally considered the most important of the three factors. The reason for this is that the business model will change, probably significantly, as the company experiments and grows. The people behind the business will have to evaluate the data, and make the decisions that will make or break the company. Execution is 99 percent of a company's success.

The market has to be big enough and growing quickly. A market that's large and growing makes it possible to build a significant company with a high valuation. This all translates into strong returns for the investor. A market that's big enough is usually at least $500 million.

Finally, investors consider the product. They want to understand its value proposition, the pain it solves, and its long-term defensibility. Traction with customers is usually the best way to demonstrate your product's worthiness from an investor's perspective.

Complete the triad to get investors excited to jump on board.

THE DAY YOU TAKE AN INVESTOR'S MONEY

L anding an investor is always exciting. Maybe you were running on fumes, only weeks away from missing a payroll, and now you can keep pressing forward. Or maybe you just nailed your customer acquisition model and this investment will allow you to really take off. Without a doubt, a capital infusion can open doors and create new possibilities. But there is one important fact you need to know before you take an investor's money—**the day you cash the check is the day you commit to selling your business.** Whether the buyer is a private company or listed on one of the public markets, the reason an investor buys a piece of your company is that she thinks she can sell it for more money down the road. Investors almost always cash out only when you sell the business.

What's more, high return requirements can put investors and entrepreneurs at odds. In extreme cases, entrepreneurs have been offered deals that would have made them millionaires, yet their investors refused to sell, holding out for a higher offer that never came.

Take on an investor only if you're comfortable with the fact that you will have to sell your company. And, when that day comes, realize that your vote won't be the only one that matters.

WHAT'S THE BUSINESS WORTH?

"**W**hat's my company worth?" This is one of an entrepreneur's most frequently asked questions. It's also one of the hardest to answer. It is possible to value a company with a fancy financial model (e.g., discounted cash flow), but the valuation will be based on projections that are little more than WAGs—Wild-Ass Guesses. **The dirty little secret is that, regardless of how sophisticated your model is, it's impossible to say exactly what an early-stage company is worth.** This is especially true with pre-revenue companies. In fact, valuation is so tricky that most seed-stage investors prefer convertible debt because it postpones the value question until the next round of financing. In the end, your company is worth whatever someone is willing to pay.

That being said, there are a few rules of thumb that should help you get to a ballpark estimate. Valuations of seed-stage investments are usually in the $1.2–$1.8 million range. VCs typically want to own 20 to 40 percent of a company in exchange for a $2–$10 million investment. To calculate the valuations of established companies with sales and profits, valuations are normally in the range of 2 to 3 times sales or 8 to 10 times profit.

If you really need an expert opinion, there are professionals who specialize in early-stage valuations and can give you an "official" estimate of your company's worth.

$1M
$1,5M
$3M
$5M
$50M
$75M
$100M

VALUATION ISN'T EVERYTHING

When it comes to choosing an investor, valuation should be just one of many selection criteria. The nonvaluation terms of a deal are also critically important. Minor changes in the deal terms can lead to wildly different economic outcomes for the founders. Work with your lawyer to watch out for terms like the liquidation preference, number of board seats, option pool, founder vesting, and type of security. Any one of these can be much more materially significant than a 20 percent difference in the valuation.

Beyond the terms of a deal, bringing on a new investor is the beginning of a long relationship. You will have to work relatively closely for years to come. Investors can be a major distraction, so working with someone who respects your time can make a big difference. Also, an investor with the right connections can open doors. Interview CEOs of the portfolio companies to get a feel for how helpful the investor is.

There's a lot to consider besides the valuation that an investor semi-arbitrarily assigns to your company. As with anything else in life, you get what you pay for. **Don't miss an opportunity to form a great alliance over a few percentage points.**

FRIENDS, FAMILY, AND FOOLS

This is the easiest money to get, and the hardest money to take.

CHAPTER 9

Building the Business

There will come a time when your business emerges from the feasibility madness and you'll have to start building the business. This happens when you stumble upon a successful business model, and you actually start making money. Often, you've been searching for the right product–market fit for so long that it doesn't feel natural to pursue only one business model, even if it's working. Consequently, you have to be very careful—if you keep searching when you should be building, you'll run out of cash.

What makes this transition even harder is that building the business calls for a completely different skill set as a manager. Just as your products have to cross the chasm with customers, your focus as a manager has to cross the chasm with internal operations.

In this chapter, you'll learn what new skills are required as a leader, how meetings kill startups, and why it's sometimes important to fire clients.

NAIL IT BEFORE YOU SCALE IT

If there is one factor that most contributes to a startup's success, it's knowing when to nail it and when to scale it. Nail the business model first, and then scale the business. Don't try to do both at once. **Invariably, winning startups figure out a profitable, repeatable business model *before* they ramp up their overhead.** It might be months (or years) before you create a business model that works, so by prematurely ramping your overhead, you sign your own death warrant. Not only does it increase the monthly cash burn rate, but more employees and divisions create a lot of unnecessary complexity.

As tempting as it may be to start hiring, anything that increases your overhead also shortens your runway. It's hard to take off from short runways. Wait to scale until you know how to consistently make profitable sales. Get a few passionate customers clamoring for your product. Wait until you know exactly how your customers think, what they need, and how to give it to them. Low overhead is the key to give your startup live a long, fruitful life.

TIPPING POINT

When you first start out, you spend half your time dreaming about how you're going to spend all of the money you make, and the other half worried that you're flushing your life savings down the drain on a harebrained idea. This sense of extreme uncertainty will stay with you until one day, when your business reaches a tipping point. It is on this day that you realize that your business is going to make it. The funny thing about the tipping point is how seemingly abrupt it is. **One day you'll be worried about paying the bills, and the next you'll wake up with a feeling of supreme confidence that your business is here to stay.**

It takes time and faith to fight through the uncertainty every entrepreneur faces. Unbelievably, most people quit on the 95-yard line. Don't let that be you. Keep believing and don't stop building. If you work hard and catch a little luck, you might wake up one day to realize that your business has tipped.

THINK ON PAPER

As an entrepreneur, you have to make dozens of decisions each and every day. Combine project management with day-to-day operations, and it's easy to get overwhelmed with details and planning. Instead of trying to juggle projects and tasks in your head, write them out and think on paper. When your tasks are no longer clogging up your thoughts, your mind will be unclouded and free to focus on the big picture.

More than the to-do's, you should also do your strategic thinking on paper. Write your ideas down, and watch them transform from nebulous and overwhelming, to tangible and actionable. **The simple act of writing out your thoughts will help you synthesize important issues, highlight critical points, and figure out the best way forward.** When you have to make an important decision, write a short memo that outlines the key points, and use it to decide the best way forward.

In addition to helping you gain clarity, thinking on paper allows you to solicit feedback from advisors and mentors. Also, you now have a written record that you can refer to in the future.

When thinking on paper, you'll find that your perception of the business is clearer and more sophisticated, which facilitates faster and better decision making.

THE FIRST QUESTION TO ASK

Small business owners are the busiest people around. They are constantly juggling dozens of projects and hundreds of tasks. The workload can become so overwhelming that it creates paralysis, confusion, or hopelessness. Any time you find yourself in this situation, break out of the funk with one question, **"If I could get only one thing done today, what would make the biggest difference in my business?"**

Ask this question first thing in the morning, before you open email or attend your first meeting, when your mind is clear and focused. Intentionally plan your day so you can focus on the company's most pressing issues.

For the question to do you any good, you have to take action. Once you determine what to do, the best thing to do is to get started on it immediately. If you can't do that, set aside some time that will allow you to focus. Ask this question for a week and you'll find that a sense of clarity and purpose has reentered your world. Ask it for a month and you'll be amazed at what you can accomplish.

MAKE MEETINGS MATTER

Meetings are for people in big companies who don't have better things to do with their time. They're one of the biggest robbers of company productivity. A pointless meeting with five people that lasts an hour is not a waste of one hour of productivity, it's a waste of five hours. On top of this, people usually hate everything about meetings. As a result, the fewer meetings you have, the more productive your organization and the happier your people.

Minimize the number of meetings at your company, and never have a meeting just for the sake of having a meeting (e.g., weekly recurring meetings). The best way to reduce the number of meetings is to start them with one simple question: What is the problem that we need this meeting to solve? If the problem you're solving doesn't require a meeting, work with people individually. The best case resulting from this question is that you realize that you don't need to have the meeting, and everyone gets back to work. The worst case is that you now have a clear justification and intended outcome for the meeting. Either way, it's a great question to get startup meetings on track.

HOPE FOR THE BEST, PLAN FOR THE WORST

It's an entrepreneur's naive optimism that leads to worries about problems that don't yet exist. The funny thing is that entrepreneurs usually worry about upside problems. But what about the downside? You have to hope for the best, and plan for the worst. **It's okay to think about scaling up, but also be prepared to scale down.** How quickly can you reduce your overhead if the orders aren't coming in as quickly as you planned? What happens if your biggest customer switches, and you lose 50 percent of your revenue? Are you able to adjust your business until you find a replacement? Make sure you create an elastic organization that can scale down as well as it can scale up. Dream big, but keep your feet planted firmly on the ground.

EXPECT THE UNEXPECTED

When it comes to building a company, you have to expect the unexpected. This is especially true for deadlines and deliverables. **Whatever you're planning, be certain that it will be harder and take longer than you expect.** That website you expected to go live in six weeks? Try six months. Raw material shipments won't show up on time, joint ventures will come together late, meetings with potential partners and investors will take forever to line up, and customers will be slow to adopt your products. When planning your strategy, factor in the unexpected.

These delays are one of the key reasons to wait as long as possible before you ramp up your overhead. You could easily and unnecessarily disadvantage yourself if you start growing too early.

Preparing for the unexpected is also important to help you deal with third-party expectations. Whether it's the press, investors, or potential customers, don't set yourself up for failure. Hold off on announcements and promises until it's already in the bag.

BE YOUR OWN CUSTOMER

The average entrepreneur works only half-time—12 hours a day. Building a company overwhelms even the most efficient and productive workers. While trying to keep up, it's easy to forget that customers are why you're here in the first place. Without a doubt, your customers should be at the top of your list of priorities. Most entrepreneurs start out taking great care of their customers, but customer attention usually suffers as a company grows. **Regardless of how busy you are, check in with your customer experience frequently.**

The best way to stay in tune with customers is to be your own customer. If you have a storefront, have a friend or secret shopper visit and report back to you. If you have a website, register as a new user and go through the complete customer life cycle. If prospects call your company to get started, make the call yourself and pretend to be a customer. While you're at it, call customer service to see how complaints are being handled. When you do this, you'll probably identify many ways to improve service. The last thing you need is more work, but your customer experience is paramount. Take time to look at your business from your customer's perspective.

THINK BIG, EXECUTE SMALL

Take time to explore game-changing possibilities. Dream big, and come up with wild ideas that can take your company to the next level. Let these big hairy audacious goals (BHAGs) inspire you. But don't let it distract you from the day-to-day execution required to build a strong company. **Building a company is about more than ideation.** Take a look around and you'll see that the world is full of people with the next big idea. **To create a lasting company, you have to execute on the fundamentals.** Look at the top athletes in the world. They don't waste much time on innovative, game-changing plays. They don't learn experimental techniques. They practice the fundamentals 99 percent of the time, because winning comes down to execution.

The chasm between those who dream and those who execute is wide and deep. Great entrepreneurs can dream big and execute fundamentals. They explore big possibilities and never stop coming up with new and better ways to do things. But they also realize that anything worthwhile takes focus, dedication, and follow-through. Think big, execute small.

FORGET THE MISSION STATEMENT

Big companies can afford to do four-day retreats in the mountains to do trust falls, sing "Kumbaya," and pay outrageously overpriced consultants to come up with impressively meaningless mission statements. You don't have this luxury. You're fighting a war with about as much hope of winning as your grandpa beating Deep Blue at chess. You can't afford a meaningless mission statement. **You need a rallying war cry that will inspire the troops to follow you on your kamikaze march. You need something actionable.** You need what Guy Kawasaki calls a "mantra." A mantra is a three- to four-word phrase that captures the heart and soul of what you're trying to accomplish. It needs to be inspirational, aspirational, and attainable—inspirational in that it moves and motivates your team to action, aspirational in that it's a meaningful and worthwhile goal, and attainable in that it's realistic and achievable. Forget the $50,000 mission statement. Spend an hour and come up with a mantra that inspires your company and makes things happen.

"It is our job to continually foster world-class infrastructures as well as to quickly create principle-centered sources to meet our customer's needs."

—*Dilbert Mission Statement Generator*

METRICS MATTER

"**What gets measured, gets managed.**" Peter Drucker's famous axiom rings true for all businesses, regardless of their size or industry. Anything that gets measured will naturally receive more attention from you and your employees. Metrics are important, quantifiable business activities. Metrics can instantly tell you how efficiently your business is operating, and make it easy to identify inefficiencies. The most common metric is the sales conversion funnel, but what you measure is limited only by your imagination.

Metrics help your company transition from a startup to a professionally managed company. Like most tools, however, they can also do more harm than good. For example, they can be time-consuming to implement effectively. They can also create an administrative burden. Resist the urge to track anything that can be measured. Find the right balance and focus your energy on a few useful metrics.

The best way to get started with metrics is to ease in. Pick your company's most important business activity, and find a good way to track and analyze it. Starting with one metric will give you a good idea of how valuable and time-consuming metrics can be. From there, continue to expand your set of metrics slowly.

YOUR NETWORK IS YOUR NET WORTH

Networking should be one of your top business-building activities. The stronger your network, the more valuable you are to your business, and to other individuals. Over time, your network will enable you to orchestrate major business deals, refer business to associates, help a friend land her next job, or even introduce future couples. Use your network to make other people successful. The more you help now, the more you'll benefit down the road. While the payoff is not immediate, your network is your net worth.

To be a mover and shaker you have to move and shake. Resolve to have at least one network development meeting every week. Make a list of your top 40 people and start reconnecting with them. When you meet new people, be sure to follow up and stay in touch. It sounds obvious, but few people actually do it.

Over the long haul, your network will be one of your most valuable assets. Creating value through your network is like any other asset—you have to invest well before you can cash out. Invest heavily. **It takes only one call to change your life, so start networking as if your future depends on it.**

　　　　　　　　　　　　　　　The Agile Startup

The Agile Startup

WHO'S THE BAD GUY?

Startups are at war. You have to outwork and outsmart the competition if you expect to win. You and your team will put in 12-hour days, week after week, year after year. It gets tiring and trying, to say the least. **To deal with all the perspiration, you and your team will need a lot of inspiration.** What inspires you and your team to work so hard, and refuse to quit against all odds? What motivates you to go the extra mile when your brain is fried and your body is begging for rest?

A surprisingly easy and effective way to get your team fired up is to identify a "bad guy." Set your sights on a direct competitor or evil empire that you and your team want to beat. This competition makes your struggle very real, because now you have a tangible enemy to aim at. You can track their activities, and use that as fodder to get your team fired up. Everybody loves the underdog story, and no one more than the underdog. Pump your team up with a little competition and get them excited about crushing the bad guy.

YOUR REPUTATION PRECEDES YOU

Your reputation is one of the few things that will stick with you forever. It's a small world, even in big cities like Los Angeles or New York. You will end up working with and running into the same people over and over again. **How you handle yourself and your business will quickly solidify your reputation in the business community.** Your reputation is very sticky, and once set, it's hard to unstick. As Warren Buffett said, "It takes 20 years to build a reputation and five minutes to ruin it. If you think about that, you'll do things differently." It only takes one or two events for your reputation to be set. As a result, make it a top priority to protect your reputation and that of your company. Protect and nurture it with the business community in the same way you handle it with your customers. Be transparent, direct, and honest. There is little adversity in the good times, so you will be judged most by how you handle yourself in the bad times. Therefore, when times get tough, dig deep and do the right thing. When in doubt, take the moral high ground. It's longer and harder, but worth the extra effort. Even if the right decision means you have to shut down your business, an untarnished reputation will allow you to bounce back quickly.

BUILD IT LIKE YOU'RE GOING TO SELL IT

Even if you have no intention of selling your business down the line, it is always smart to begin with the end and build it as if you are going to sell it. On the winding road of life, you never know what lies around the next curve. Your situation could change drastically in the future, so it's always better to have the option to sell. What does *build it like you're going to sell it* mean? More than anything else, this means taking yourself out of the picture. **The less dependent the business is on you, the more valuable it will be to someone else.** Businesses that depend on the founder are usually not sellable. You may be the rainmaker now, but reduce your burden by hiring other rainmakers. Get yourself out of the picture and build an organization that can sustain itself. This way, even if you never end up selling the business, it can provide the lifestyle you hoped for when you first started out.

BE FRUGAL, NOT CHEAP

Cash is always tight in a startup, so you have to watch every penny that goes out the door. **But there comes a point when frugal turns into cheap, and you end up doing more harm than good.** By skimping on certain expenses, you could seriously hinder your business's ability to perform or to expand.

Entrepreneurs are notorious for trying to do everything themselves. Taxes are a great example of being too cheap. Rather than paying a bookkeeper $50 a month, founders often try to do their taxes themselves. Not only does it take them forever to learn Quickbooks and add the necessary entries, but they're usually wrong.

There are two things you should do to be frugal and not cheap. First, make a monthly or quarterly budget of projected expenses. By doing this in advance, as part of a larger strategy session, you take the emotion out of the decision making, and do what's best for the business. Second, especially when it comes to larger capital investments, do a back-of-the-envelope payback period calculation. Figure out how long it will take to earn back your initial investment. This payback period should give you an idea as to whether the proposed expense will be worthwhile.

Be careful not to be too cheap. Otherwise, as Henry Ford said, "If you need a machine and then don't buy it, you'll eventually find you paid for it but don't own it."

The Agile Startup

WHEN THE S#!T HITS THE FAN (AND IT WILL)

When building your company, you will inevitably have a number of "it's over" moments. A moment like this happens when things have become so dire and hopeless that closing up shop seems like it's your only viable option. Every entrepreneur goes through this. In startups, these near-death experiences are so commonplace that surviving one is a rite of passage. After a while, you will become hardened to these kinds of shocks. People you work with will wonder how you hold it together when the world seems to be crumbling around you. **There's only one thing that matters, and that's not what happens to you. All that matters is how you respond.** So get mad for a few minutes if you want to. Then, after the initial shock of the third "catastrophe" this week wears off, regroup and figure out next steps. You've got work to do.

KNOW WHEN TO FOLD 'EM

Without a doubt, perseverance is a core characteristic of every successful entrepreneur. **You'll never make it in the startup racket if you can't push through some adversity. But there's a difference between intelligent and insane perseverance.** Not every business is long for this world. If you've got a loser on your hands, there's no point in dying a slow, painful death. If you find yourself in a hole, stop digging! Cut it loose and move on.

How do you know when to fold 'em? There's no easy answer to this question. The only practical advice—that you probably won't follow because it's the hardest thing for a passionate entrepreneur to do—is to make sure that you don't dig yourself into such a deep hole that you can't get out. In other words, don't invest all of your retirement savings and home equity into your business. Make sure that you have a safety net. It's intelligent to be financially committed, but insane to have your entire net worth on the line. It's better to lose the battle and still have a shot at winning the war.

Another important piece of advice—if you do have to shut down, realize that there's no shame in it. Serial entrepreneurs invariably say they learned a lot more from their failures than their successes. Take the lessons you learned and use them to make your next company even better.

CHAPTER 10

What to Know Before You Go

Dedicating your life to starting a company is serious business. It's a hard, lonely, and severe journey that's not for everyone. Unfortunately, most people jump into entrepreneurship without really understanding what they're getting into. Your startup is going to take everything you've got (and then some), which means you'll work around the clock. Weekends? What weekends? Those are gone also. Consequently, your family and social life will take major hits, as you won't have the time or money to maintain your current lifestyle. You're on your own to sink or swim, and if you don't sell, then your family doesn't eat. The pressure can crush the average person.

This chapter sheds light on what to anticipate before you dive in head first, how to set yourself up for success, and what questions you should ask so you can understand what you're about to get yourself into.

The Agile Startup

STARTUPS ARE BORING

Entrepreneurs are the new rock stars. The press loves to write about high-profile entrepreneurs and the latest acquisitions or IPOs. Unfortunately, $100 million IPOs, private jets, and celebrity parties are not the life of the typical entrepreneur. On the contrary, startups are boring: **98 percent of the work done in a startup is monotonous and painstaking.**

Part of the reason for this misconception is that the ideation phase is the most exciting time of a startup's life. When you're first starting out, the sky is the limit. Reality doesn't matter because you're just dreaming. Do you have customers? Who knows, and who cares? "Don't bother me with details." It's after the initial ideation phase that startups get boring. This is when the struggle begins. This is when it gets hard, and the real entrepreneurs come out.

Startups aren't all sunshine and rainbows, so don't get fooled by the media. Reporters are great at selling fantasies, but real entrepreneurs don't live in fantasyland. Be ready to do the grunge work before you turn your life upside down and try to become the next rock star entrepreneur.

YOUNG AT HEART

T hink you're too old to start a business? Think again—the average age of an entrepreneur is 39 years old. The Kauffman Foundation study that documented this average age also found that entrepreneurial activity is consistent across all ages. Contrary to the 20-something entrepreneurs that the mass media glorifies, people of all ages, educations, and backgrounds start businesses. Look no further than Colonel Sanders who started Kentucky Fried Chicken at the age of 65 with an investment from the Social Security Administration—his first benefits check.

No, you don't need to be young to start a business. You don't need to be well-off, either. Think about the legions of immigrants who came to America, didn't speak English, and didn't have a penny, yet became wildly successful. **While your physical age and resources don't matter, your emotional age and resourcefulness do.** You have to be young at heart to start a company because it takes boundless energy and dedication. If you can't put in the effort, you're better off starting a new hobby instead. As good as Colonel Sanders' chicken was, he got rejected more than 1,000 times before he signed his first franchisee. Now that's young at heart.

YOUR THREE HATS

It's easy to get frustrated working for someone else. You probably do the work better than your employer, which begs the question—why not go out on your own? As tempting as this may be, know what you're getting into before you jump ship. Regardless of the industry, **there are three distinct hats that every business owner must wear: technician, manager, and entrepreneur.** The technician is the person who does the work of the business. In an architecture firm, for example, the technician is the person who creates the blueprints. The second two hats are usually overlooked by aspiring businessowners. The manager runs the business on a day-to-day basis. This is mostly mind-numbing busywork that everyone hates to do. The third hat is the entrepreneur who innovates and drives sales.

You have to wear all three hats when you run your own business. Ironically, there's often so much work for the manager and entrepreneur that the technical work that you love to do gets pushed aside. Before you take the plunge, realize what's required to build the business. When push comes to shove, you might be happier as a technician.

YOU ARE ON YOUR OWN

One of the hardest things about starting a company is that you are on your own. Who can you turn to for help and advice with challenges? You can't talk to employees, who, upon hearing there is only a month's worth of cash left in the bank, will immediately start sending out resumes. It's hard to be totally upfront with investors, who you will probably ask for more money down the road. As great as mentors can be, most issues would take too long to get them fully up to speed. Unfortunately, there's no easy solution. **Isolation and total responsibility are the burdens in the life of the CEO and entrepreneur.** The best you can do is to minimize your isolation as much as possible. Surround yourself with highly capable and intelligent people who can help shoulder the load. Keep a journal that you use to organize your thoughts over time. Keep in close contact with your advisory board, which can help with key strategic decisions. Consider joining an organization like Vistage, which hosts roundtables with other CEOs that can act as a sounding board. Usually, small things like these can go a long way to help reduce the pressure and keep you on track.

DANGERS IN THE MOONLIGHT

A common way to get your startup going is to keep your full-time job, and be an entrepreneur on the side. This can be smart, or it can be incredibly stupid, depending on your current employer. When you first start a job, you sign a lot of contracts. If you read the fine print, you'll see that the employer almost always retains intellectual property rights. This means **that your employer might own the rights to your ideas—even those you think up in your spare time.** In a moonlighting entrepreneur's worst nightmare, it's not inconceivable for your previous employer to sue you, claiming that it owns the rights to your invention or company. Annoyingly, they'll usually come after you only after you're successful and fought through the risk. Obviously, this is a situation that you want to avoid. Before you moonlight, ask a lawyer to read through your employment agreements. Make sure that you will own your company free and clear when you decide to take the leap. Even then, don't use your employer's resources to build your company. It can come back to bite you.

THE PART-TIME ENTREPRENEUR

It's always debatable whether you should start out as a full-time entrepreneur or keep your job and work on your startup on the side. Starting a company in your spare time significantly reduces your risk and opportunity cost. But, if the deck weren't already stacked against you, succeeding on a part-time basis is *a lot* more difficult than doing so full time. When your company is a part-time project, your business will be hard to prioritize consistently, your competition will run circles around you, you'll miss opportunities, and—most importantly—your back won't be against the wall. If you have the stability of a full-time job, it's much harder to get out of your comfort zone and do what it takes to get the job done.

It only makes sense to work on an idea part-time when you want to study its feasibility. When it becomes apparent that you have a winner on your hands, your best bet is to dive in headfirst. There's just no way around it—you have to dedicate everything you've got to your startup. This is especially true for investors. If you want to be taken seriously, you have to be serious about your business. And that means quitting your job and building this business full-time.

A FAMILY AFFAIR

You already know that starting a business is an all-consuming pursuit. What you may not realize is that it will consume your family as well. Starting a business is truly a family affair. To one degree or another, everyone will have to step up and make sacrifices. Your income will decrease significantly for the foreseeable future, which means you won't be able to afford many luxuries. Instead of leisure time, your family will probably end up putting in time on your business. You will be working throughout most of your kids' childhoods.

Startups have broken up many happy homes, so set expectations from the beginning. Make sure your significant other is 100 percent on board, and ready to make the necessary sacrifices. Starting a business usually does one of two things: It brings you closer together or drives you apart. Make sure your relationship can withstand the stresses of a startup. Address any hesitation or trepidation up front, with an open and honest discussion. Your family's unwavering support will be critical to overcome the challenges that you'll inevitably face.

CONGRATULATIONS, IT'S A BOY!

Founding a company is like having a baby. It takes just as much time, energy, and attention. Like raising a child, your startup is a direct reflection of you, and it's up to you to make sure that it has the right values and mission. You have to protect it when it's young, and help it grow up to be strong and independent. You pour your heart and soul into it, and will do anything to make it succeed. It sucks your bank accounts dry and you gladly pay.

If you have a business partner, it's like having a spouse. In fact, in the early years you will likely spend more waking hours with your partner than your spouse.

Like parenthood, owning a business is also one of the most rewarding things you can do. To watch your business grow into a powerhouse is amazing and inspiring. To see that you created something where before there was nothing, to know that you made your own little dent in the universe, creates an unparalleled feeling of pride and satisfaction.

Before you get started, recognize that starting a company is a serious commitment. If you are going to succeed, it will take the same dedication and lifestyle rearrangement as parenthood. Are you sure you're ready to bring a baby into this world?

TEN THINGS YOU SHOULD NEVER DO BEFORE STARTING

Whatever you do,

1. Don't write a business plan—this comes later.
2. Don't try to get a loan—you won't qualify anyway.
3. Don't start building immediately—get feedback first.
4. Don't rent an office—work from home.
5. Don't advertise—what would you advertise, anyway?
6. Don't buy fancy equipment—rent or borrow; save your cash.
7. Don't quit your job—there's a lot of setup you can do first.
8. Don't incorporate—worry about this distraction later.
9. Don't look for a partner—explore the idea first.
10. Don't hire employees—start building it yourself.

These are fatal mistakes that can doom your startup from the beginning. They are either major distractions that pull your focus away from what matters, or they're a waste of your precious startup capital. Put first things first, and avoid these ten temptations.

THE FIVE-YEAR OVERNIGHT SUCCESS

what people think
it looks like

what it really
looks like

Conclusion

And there you have it—170 quick and dirty lessons that every entrepreneur should know. Follow these strategies to avoid sleepless nights, prevent ulcers, and make your startup journey generally less painful.

There are a few common themes throughout the book that are worth highlighting. These strategies cut across all stages of the entrepreneur's life cycle. They form the core of the Agile Startup philosophy, and winning entrepreneurs understand them innately. Find ways to incorporate these themes into your own startup strategy.

In no particular order, they are:

- The name of the startup game is to reduce your risk by turning assumptions into facts as quickly as possible. Assumptions and survival are inversely correlated—the more assumptions you make, the less likely you'll survive.

- At least a few of your key assumptions are dead wrong, so go talk to the people who have the answers.

- When in doubt, act. You don't know enough yet to waste time thinking and planning.

- The team is the most important piece of the startup puzzle. It's also one of the hardest to get right.

- The next most important piece is the market. If you can find an underserved niche in a large and growing market, then half of the work is already done for you.

- Nail the business model before you start scaling the business. Prematurely building your overhead expenses before solidifying your business model is one of the most common startup killers.

- It's hard to find meaningful differentiation, and harder to build barriers to entry. Try anyway.

- It's not a startup until you build something, and it's not a business until you sell something.

- You must FOCUS as an entrepreneur, and in all aspects of your business. Unless you want a war story about how your startup crashed and burned, stay focused on the most important activities.

- Never forget Rule #1, and have fun. After all, if you're not having fun, what's the point?

Be sure to visit *www.agilestartup.com*, where we post new startup strategies. Also, you can sign up for our free newsletter that's packed with the latest and greatest tools and tactics for entrepreneurs.

Good luck!

Acknowledgments

Many of the lessons in this book are a direct result of the experiences of my professional career. There are hundreds of people whose impact on my professional career have shaped this book. To Packard Bell, Kistler Aerospace, Ardica Technologies, Tornado Development, Channel M, and countless others: I extend my appreciation for your generous support and invaluable impact.

I would like to extend a special thank-you to the UCLA Anderson School of Management and the Price Center for Entrepreneurial Studies for allowing me the opportunity to contribute. Through the guidance of Al Osborne, the Senior Associate Dean, and Elaine Hagan, the Director of the Price Center, I have grown as an educator. It has been an honor to teach alongside such esteemed faculty and work with an institution that is so committed to enriching the minds of tomorrow's entrepreneurs.

Thanks to Originate for allowing me the flexibility to pursue my passion as an educator. My partners and team members have supported me tremendously throughout my journey.

Finally, I send my deepest gratitude to Marlene, who has endured my grouchiness and all-too-frequent unavailability. Her unmatched support and patience have provided me with a solid foundation that I can always depend on.

—Jeff Scheinrock

The Agile Startup was a blast from the beginning. Everything about the book, from setting up the website in 2009 to escaping to the woods to write in 2012, has been an adventure that I'll always remember.

Thanks to John Wiley & Sons for making all of this possible. Thanks to my parents, Kathy and Bob Richter-Sand. I wouldn't be here if it wasn't for their unwavering support and encouragement. They both strive for excellence in their personal and professional lives and serve as a constant source of inspiration for me. Thanks to Jeff for being such a great mentor and co-author. Thanks to UCLA Anderson School of Management for opening the world of business to me, and starting me down the entrepreneurial path. Finally, thanks to all of my business partners over the years, who have taught me so much about startups and life. Many of the lessons in this book I owe to them.

—Matt Richter-Sand

Recommended Reading

The following authors, entrepreneurs, and investors have blazed the trail to make *The Agile Startup* possible. In no particular order, the following books, articles, and blogs are highly recommended reading. The author's writings, philosophies, and methodologies are referenced throughout *The Agile Startup*.

- Steve Blank
  - Blog—*http://steveblank.com/*
  - Book—*The Startup Owner's Manual: The Step-by-Step Guide for Building a Great Company* by Steve Blank and Bob Dorf (Pescadero, CA: K&S Ranch Press, 2012)
- Brad Feld
  - Blog—Feld Thoughts—*www.feld.com/wp/*
  - Book—*Venture Deals: Be Smarter Than Your Lawyer and Venture Capitalist* by Brad Feld, Jason Mendelson, and Dick Costolo (Hoboken, NJ: John Wiley & Sons, 2012)
- Guy Kawasaki
  - Blog—*http://blog.guykawasaki.com/*
  - Book—*The Art of the Start: The Time-Tested, Battle-Hardened Guide for Anyone Starting Anything* by Guy Kawasaki (New York: Penguin Group, 2004)
- Eric Ries
  - Blog—*www.startuplessonslearned.com/*

- Book—*The Lean Startup: How Today's Entrepreneurs Use Continuous Innovation to Create Radically Successful Businesses* by Eric Ries (New York: Crown Business, 2011)
- Mark Suster
  - Blog—*www.bothsidesofthetable.com/*
- Alexander Osterwalder
  - Book—*Business Model Generation: A Handbook for Visionaries, Game Changers, and Challengers* by Alexander Osterwalder and Yves Pigneur (Hoboken, NJ: John Wiley & Sons, 2010)
- Peter Drucker
  - Book—*Innovation and Entrepreneurship* by Peter F. Drucker (New York: HarperCollins, 2006)
- Geoffrey Moore
  - Book—*Crossing the Chasm: Marketing and Selling Disruptive Products to Mainstream Customers* by Geoffrey A. Moore and Regis McKenna (New York: HarperCollins, 2002)
- Seth Godin
  - Blog—*http://sethgodin.typepad.com/*

About the Authors

JEFF SCHEINROCK

Jeff Scheinrock is currently a Continuing Lecturer at UCLA Anderson School of Management, and President and Partner at Originate (*Originate.com*). A pioneer in venture resources, Originate invests capital and elite engineering resources in high potential early-stage companies. Prior to Originate, Jeff was the Chief Investment Officer of GKM Newport Generation Funds, which invested in excess of $950 million in venture capital and private equity buyout funds. Before that, Jeff served as Vice Chairman, Chief Financial Officer, and Director of Kistler Aerospace Corporation, where he successfully raised $350 million. From 1989 to 1996, Jeff served as Vice Chairman of Finance and Strategic Planning for Packard Bell NEC Electronics, Inc. There, he set up operations throughout Europe and Asia, and negotiated in excess of $1 billion in bank debt and $3 billion in trade credit. He also handled the negotiation and structuring of all acquisitions including Zenith Data Systems and Ark Interface Software among others. Prior to joining Packard Bell NEC, Jeff was CPA and Senior Partner in charge of the Entrepreneurial Services Group of Arthur Young, a Big 8 accounting firm.

MATT RICHTER-SAND

Matt Richter-Sand has an extensive background in technology and entrepreneurship. After graduating from Tulane University with degrees in computer science, mathematics, and political science, he joined the U.S. Air Force as a Communications Officer. While stationed at Edwards Air Force Base in California, Matt was responsible for all core IT services for 11,000 on-base personnel.

After a brief stint in Corporate America, Matt decided to pursue his passion for entrepreneurship full time. He began consulting with entrepreneurs and investing in early-stage companies at Originate, and starting companies of his own. Matt has previously started three businesses. One was a "lesson learned," one was acquired, and he's in the midst of his third company, an online fitness program.

Matt earned a masters in business administration from UCLA Anderson School of Management in 2010, and currently teaches courses in entrepreneurship at UCLA Extension.

Online Course Offer

TURN YOUR IDEA INTO A BUSINESS IN 13 STEPS

Jeff Scheinrock and Matt Richter-Sand, authors of *The Agile Startup*, have created an online course that shows you exactly what you need to do to turn your "million dollar" idea into a thriving business. The course is a comprehensive system that covers the 13 steps you need to take to get your business off the ground. The 13 steps are:

1. Get the *Philosophy and Mindset* of a great entrepreneur
2. Create a *Product or Service* with a killer value proposition
3. Determine *Feasibility* of the idea
4. Figure out how to make money with the *Business Model*
5. Break down the *Market*
6. Analyze the *Competition*
7. Create an effective *Marketing Plan*
8. Assemble a powerful *Team*
9. Analyze your *Financials* and build a financial model

10. Learn effective *Pitch and Sales* techniques

11. Understand your options on *Funding Your Startup*

12. Get your *Legal, Taxes, and IP* squared away

13. *Build the Business* by setting it up for growth

Get 25 percent off the course by using the code 1A8AU3W5M.

In addition to the course content, when you sign up you will receive more than $400 of bonuses.

Learn more and get started today at *www.agilestartup.com/training*.

Index